STUDY GUIDE TO ACCOMPANY SENNA & SIEGEL'S

THIRD EDITION

INTRODUCTION TO CRIMINAL JUSTICE

Prepared by
Roy Roberg
Administration of Justice Department
San Jose State University

WEST PUBLISHING COMPANY
St. Paul New York Los Angeles San Francisco

50 West Kellogg Boulevard
P.O. Box 3526
St. Paul, MN 55165

Printed in the United States of America
ISBN 0-314-77793-8

Contents

STUDENT INTRODUCTION

This study guide has been designed and written to introduce students to the field of criminal justice by helping them to master the important concepts and principles presented in the third edition to Introduction to Criminal Justice, and to further stimulate interest in defining the problems and solutions which confront the administration of justice system. Following is a brief description of *how* this workbook should be utilized in preparing for examinations.

Included in the workbook are five major sections: Key Terms and Concepts; Fill-In Review; Self-Test; Essay Questions; and an Answer Section. It is suggested that before you begin to read the text, you familiarize yourself with the key terms and concepts listed in the first section. In this way, the identity of major terms and key points should become familiar to you as you read through each chapter.

The Fill-In Review section has been prepared to give you immediate feedback as to your knowledge of the material presented in the text. After each chapter has been read and studied, an attempt should be made to write in the correct word, phrase, or case in the blank spaces provided, without the use of the test for reference. After this section has been completed, you can evaluate your accuracy by turning to the Answer Section at the back of the chapter. If you have problems completing some of the fill-in questions, the text should be reviewed until all the answers can be provided. In order to assist you in locating the correct responses, this section has been prepared in sequential order with the material in the text.

After you have thoroughly studied for the examination, you should answer the questions in the Self-Test section (on each chapter which will be covered), as if you were actually taking the exam. This section contains True-False,

Multiple Choice, Matching, and Essay questions; although most exams in introductory courses tend to be primarily multiple choice in nature, the other types of questions in this section will help you to assess your knowledge of the materials.

It is believed that if you can respond correctly to a high percentage of the sample test questions in this workbook, you will be well prepared for objective and/or essay examinations on the text material. It should be noted that questions in the Self-Test section have been "scrambled" and are not presented in the same order as the text material. If you respond incorrectly to a high percentage of the questions, you most likely will not do well on an actual exam; you should then intensify your study of the materials in the textbook as well as review the study guide.

CHAPTER ONE

CRIME IN AMERICA

KEY TERMS AND CONCEPTS

Criminology
Criminal Justice
Crime
Consensus View
Social Control
Interactionist View
Social Power
Conflict View
Economic Power
Decriminalize
Federal Bureau of Investigation
Uniform Crime Reports (UCR)
Index Crimes
Murder
Victim-Precipitated Murder
Forcible Rape
Aggravated Assault
Robbery
Burglary
Larceny/Theft
Motor Vehicle Theft
Arson
Victimization Studies
National Crime Survey
Self-Report Studies

FILL-IN REVIEW

1. One of the basic goals of our society is to develop an understanding of the ____________ of ____________ and to identify and implement plans for its elimination.

2. ____________ is the study of crime, its causes and control whereas ____________ ____________ is the study of how the American system of justice functions.

3. According to the ____________ view, crimes are behaviors that are essentially harmful to a ____________ of citizens living in society and have been controlled or ____________ by the existing criminal law.

4. The ____________ view of crime holds that the criminal law is influenced by people who hold ____________ ____________ and use it to hold the law to reflect their way of thinking.

5. The ____________ view of crime maintains that the true purpose of the criminal law is to protect the ____________ of the upper classes at the expense of the poor.

6. Crime can be defined as a political, social and ____________ function of modern life.

7. Criminal law is a ____________ code that represents the influence of a number of sources, each attempting to control public ____________ through control of the law.

8. The Uniform ____________ ____________ are the best known and most widely cited source of criminal statistics.

9. Basically, Part II offenses, while excluding traffic violations, include all other crimes except those classified as ____________ ____________ offenses.

10. Violent crimes reported by the FBI include ____________, rape, assault, and ____________.

11. ____________ is one of the most underreported of all crimes.

12. A murder in which the victim's behavior is often an important factor is termed a ______-______ homicide.

13. Property crimes reported by the FBI include burglary, ____________, motor vehicle theft, and ____________.

14. ____________ is by far the most common crime reported to the FBI.

15. ____________ was added to the ____________ crime category in 1979 since it is now considered one of the nation's most serious crime patterns.

16. Over the years, the FBI estimates that about ____________ percent of all Index Crimes are ____________ by arrest.

17. Two major problems with the UCR's are citizen neglect to ____________ criminal acts to police and variations in ____________ ____________ practices.

18. According to victimization studies, fewer than ____________ of all crimes are actually ____________ to the police.

19. National Crime Survey data show that members of the lowest income categories were by far the most likely victims of ___________ crimes and most personal ___________ crimes.

20. Self-report studies suggest that crime is much ___________ common than either official or victimization studies would lead us to believe.

SELF-TEST

True-False

1. The fear of crime has been accentuated by a lack of faith in the government.

2. The meaning of the term "crime" is consistent and unchanging, with no variation.

3. According to the consensus view of crime, the criminal law has a social control function.

4. The conflict position of crime differs from the interactionist view because it has a distinctly political orientation.

5. The UCR employs two basic methods to employ crime data.

6. Victim-precipitated homicides, the victim's behavior is usually not an important factor.

7. Robbery was one of the few Index Crimes that rose significantly between 1980 and 1981.

8. NCS data show that members of the middle income categories are by far the most likely to be victims of violent crimes.

9. According to Quinney, the ability to confer criminal status is a privilege enjoyed by the propertied classes and suffered by the non-propertied.

10. One of the stated objectives of the National Advisory Commission on Criminal Justice Standards and Goals is a reduction of one-half of the current robbery rate.

11. The victim of both power and anger rapes tends to be of the same age group as the offender.

12. The majority of murders are committed with a blunt object.

13. Aggravated assaults have increased steadily since the 1960's due, most likely, to civil disobedience, turmoil, and assassinations occuring in the time frame.

14. U.S. citizens are believed to report less than one-half of all criminal and delinquent acts to police.

15. Like the UCR, the NCS and all other victim surveys suffer from some methodological problems.

16. Self-report studies measure the so-called "dark figures" of crime.

17. The female arrest rate has been increasing at a faster rate than that of the male.

Multiple Choice

1. The major unit of analysis in the Uniform Crime Reports are:
   a. index crimes
   b. appendix crimes
   c. Part I offenses
   d. both a and c

2. According to recent figures of the UCR's, the majority of burglaries occured in:
   a. personal residences
   b. business establishments
   c. motor vehicles
   d. non-residential property

3. The unlawful taking or stealing of property without the use of force, violence, or fraud constitutes:
   a. burglary
   b. robbery
   c. larceny/theft
   d. simple-theft

4. Which of the following is <u>not</u> considered an Index Crime of the Uniform Crime Reports:
   a. non-negligent manslaughter
   b. murder
   c. robbery
   d. assault and battery

5. Which of the following is <u>not</u> an element or part of the crime of burglary:
   a. use of force
   b. unlawful entry of a structure
   c. intent to commit a felony or theft
   d. all are needed to define a crime as a burglary

6. Which of the following views of crime agree that the criminal law defines crime, but challenges the belief that the law represents the opinion of a majority of citizens:
   a. conflict view
   b. consensus view
   c. interactionist view
   d. none of the above

7. The FBI estimates that about ____________ percent of all Index Crimes are cleared by arrest.
   a. 10%
   b. 20%
   c. 40%
   d. 50%

8. If the UCR indicates that the murder rate was 9.8 in 1981, it means about 10 people in every ____________ fell victim to murder between January 1 and December 31, of 1981.
   a. 1,000
   b. 10,000
   c. 100,000
   d. 1,000,000

9. Self-report studies:
   a. suggest that crime is more common than official (UCR) studies indicate
   b. suggest that crime is more common than victimization (NCS) studies indicate
   c. ask offenders to tell about their own criminal activities
   d. all of the above

10. Stealing or taking of anything of value from the care or control of a person by force or violence or by putting in fear constitutes a:
    a. burglary
    b. robbery
    c. aggravated assault
    d. larceny

11. In defining an aggravated assault, the perpetrator of the crime must have the intent to:
    a. inflict severe bodily injury
    b. inflict aggravated bodily injury
    c. kill
    d. both a and b

12. Criminology is the study of:
    a. crime causation
    b. crime control
    c. crime and its control
    d. crime, its causation and control

13. The most common crime reported by the FBI is:
    a. homicide
    b. robbery
    c. larceny/theft
    d. rape

14. A critical element of Richard Quinney's theory of crime is that:
    a. crime must be punished
    b. crime is created by ruling authorities
    c. crime is inherent behavior
    d. crime is committed by the powerless

15. Which of the following is <u>not</u> considered to be a property crime included in the UCR:
    a. burglary
    b. larceny
    c. arson
    d. all of the above are considered property crimes of the UCR

Matching

1.	S. Schafer and R. Knudten	A.	"The formal legal definition of crime upholds the principle that no crime exists unless it is so defined by the law (<u>nullum crimen sine lege</u>)"
2.	E. Sutherland and C. Cressy	B.	Criminal behavior is behavior in violation of the criminal law... it is not a crime unless it is prohibited by the criminal law.
3.	Ramsey Clark	C.	"Powerless people live by their wits... The law is irrelevant except when it comes after them or their loved ones."
4.	Richard Quinney	D.	Crime is not "inherent in behavior, but is a judgement made by some about the actions and characteristics of others."

ESSAY QUESTIONS

1. Make up your own definition of crime and discuss the problems associated with such a definition.

2. Discuss several reasons why the Uniform Crime Reports are unreliable.

3. What seems to be the future trend of collecting and disseminating criminological statistics? What will be the significance of these methods?

4. Discuss whether or not you believe crime rates will continue to decline throughout the 1980's; give several specific reasons.

CHAPTER 1 ANSWER SECTION

FILL-IN REVIEW

1. causes, crimes
2. Criminology, Criminal Justice
3. consensus, majority, prohibited
4. interactionist, social, power
5. conflict, power
6. economic
7. legal, behavior
8. Crime Reports
9. Part I
10. murder, robbery
11. Rape
12. victim-precipitated
13. larceny, arson
14. Larceny/theft
15. Arson, index
16. 20, cleared
17. report, law enforcement
18. half, reported
19. violent, theft
20. more

SELF-TEST

True-False

1\. True
1\. False
3\. True
4\. True
5 False
6\. False
7\. True
8\. False
9\. True
10\. True
11\. False
12\. False
13\. True
14\. True
15\. True
16\. True
17\. True

Multiple Choice

1. (d) both a and c
2. (a) personal residences
3. (c) larceny/theft
4. (d) assault and battery
5. (a) use of force
6. (c) interactionist view
7. (b) 20%
8. (c) 100,000
9. (d) all of the above
10. (b) robbery
11. (d) both a and b above
12. (d) crime, its causation and control
13. (c) larceny/theft
14. (b) crime is created by ruling authorities
15. (d) all of the above are considered property crimes of the UCR

Matching

1. A
2. B
3. C
4. D

CHAPTER TWO

UNDERSTANDING CRIME AND ITS CAUSES

KEY TERMS AND CONCEPTS

Survey Research
Observation Studies
Participant Observation
Life Histories
Record Studies
Classical Theories
General Deterrence
Incapacitation
Special Deterrence
Positivist Theories
Cesare Lombroso
Sociobiology
47XYY Syndrome
Psychological Theories
Sigmund Freud
Sociological Theories
Emile Durkheim
Anomie
Robert Merton
Albert Cohen
Delinquent Gang Theory
R. Cloward & L. Ohlin
Opportunity Theory
Walter Miller
Lower Class Culture Theory
Social Process Theories
Edwin Sutherland
Differential Association
D. Matza & G. Sykes
Neutralization Theory
Travis Hirschi
Social Bond Theory
Labeling Theory
Social Conflict Theory
Female Criminality
Juvenile Delinquent

FILL-IN REVIEW

1. Criminology is the ____________ study of ____________, the characteristics of criminals and the prevention of criminality.

2. ____________ sampling assumes that the characteristics of the small select sample group mirror those of the larger ____________ from which the sample group is drawn.

3. ____________ observation is the type of research where the ____________ joins the group being studied and behaves as a member of the group.

4. The first organized view of crime causation is known today as ____________ theory.

5. Studies showing the relationship between sanctions and crime rates have failed to generate data sufficient to demonstrate that increasing ____________ will always decrease ____________ behaviors.

6. ____________ refers to the belief that dangerous criminal offenders should be locked away for ____________ periods of time.

7. Positivistic theories of criminality agrue that behavior is ____________ by who we are and the world we live in.

8. Sociobiology views all human behavior as a function of a person's ____________ makeup; the ____________ in which the person lives; and ____________ potential and experiences.

9. Psychological approaches of crime can be divided into four significant areas of study: the ____________ view, the ____________ view, the ____________ view and the ____________ view.

10. ____________ means the absence or weakness of rules and social norms in any person or group.

11. Some socioculture theorists postulate that lower-class citizens form a separate "____________", maintaining unique values clashing with those held by the middle class.

12. Lower-class culture theory maintains that the criminal behavior found in working class ghetto areas is common, due to the unique ____________ structure which prevails there.

13. ____________ ____________ theories view criminal behavior as a function of an individual's life experiences; conversely ____________ theories view criminal behavior as a function of social class conflicts.

14. The best known American theory of adult criminality is ____________ ____________, which is primarily a ____________ theory.

15. Neutralization theory portrays delinquents as adhering to ____________ values while "____________" into episodic instances of illegal behavior.

16. Hirschi eludes to the proposition that a person's social bond is weakened by two main sources: disrupted ____________ life, and poor ____________ ability.

17. The ____________ theory views society as creating deviance through a system of social control agencies, which are designed to designate certain individuals as ____________.

18. ___________ criminology views the criminal law and criminal justice system as vehicles for ___________ the poor, have-not, members of society.

19. ___________ criminology focuses on the evils of capitalism and attempts to expose the crime-producing forces inherent in our free ___________ system.

20. Criminologists have traditionally devoted little time or effort to studying the ___________ role in the crime problem.

21. Recent self-report data suggest that the relationship between male and female ___________ is closer than previously believed.

22. The most significant development of juvenile crime has been the widespread use of ___________ and ___________.

SELF-TEST

True-False

1. There is a great deal of overlap between the study of criminology and criminal justice.

2. Observation studies always include participant observation.

3. Classical theory suggests that people will not commit crimes because of their fear of criminal sanctions.

4. The concept of general deterrence does not assume rationality on the part of the offender.

5. Multiple-cause theories of crime have none of the problems which plague single-cause approaches.

6. Quetelet developed the theory of anomie, meaning the absence or weakness of rules and social norms in any person or group.

7. According to Merton's theory of anomie, a person with a retreatism orientation has rejected conventional societal goals and means and substituted alternatives to them.

8. Special deterrence refers to the belief that dangerous criminal offenders should be locked away for long periods of time.

9. Biological explanations of criminal behavior are once again generating interest.

10. Opportunity theory suggests that even opportunities for criminal gain are closed or "blocked" to many citizens.

11. The "war on poverty" social and economic improvement projects in the 1960's and 1970's, such as the Job Corp Vocational Training Program, received impetus from Cloward and Ohlin's Opportunity Theory.

12. Miller has been able to point to countless incidents to substantiate the existence of the so-called lower-class culture.

13. The basic principle of differential association is that individuals learn criminal behavior when definitions of law violations exceed those that support conformity.

14. Neutralization theory has been tested empirically, providing clear authentication of its major principles.

15. Labeling theory portrays criminality as a political rather than a moral function.

16. According to labeling theory, an individual may at first commit a relatively harmless act, and subsequently be transformed into a career deviant due to societal action.

17. Sociobiological theories have been the predominant view in criminology for most of the twentieth century.

18. Marxist criminology views crime as a product of class conflict.

19. While boys are more delinquent than girls, males and females generally engage in the same delinquent behavior.

Multiple Choice

1. The proponent of the view that crime is an intrinsic part of a society and a function of its internal conflict, was:
   a. Cesare Lombroso
   b. Walter Miller
   c. Emile Durkheim
   d. Robert Merton

2. Which of the following criminological methods uses information obtained from probability samples:
   a. survey research
   b. record studies
   c. observation studies
   d. life histories

3. The effectiveness of general deterrence appears to be limited by:
   a. the efficiency of the justice system
   b. it assumes rationality on the part of the offender
   c. the elaborate array of legal rights in our system
   d. all of the above limit the effectiveness of general deterrence

4. The origins of modern criminological thought are found in the biophysical theories of:
   a. Henry Maudsly
   b. Raffaele Garofalo
   c. Enrico Ferri
   d. Cesare Lombroso

5. The concept that the pains of imprisonment should be so severe that on release convicted offenders will not dare repeat their criminal acts is:
   a. incapacitation
   b. special deterrence
   c. general deterrence
   d. both a and b

6. One area of ___________ psychology which is of particular interest to criminology is the identification of the psychopathic personality.
   a. psychoanalytic
   b. physiological
   c. cognitive
   d. behavioral

7. Which of the following is <u>not</u> a social process theory:
   a. opportunity theory
   b. neutralization theory
   c. social bond theory
   d. labeling theory

8. Hirschi's social bond theory does <u>not</u> include within its scope:
   a. attachment
   b. belief
   c. commitment
   d. appeal

9. According to labeling theory, the labeling process begins:
   a. upon conviction
   b. upon sentencing
   c. "getting caught"
   d. when released from custody

10. Delinquent behavior:
    a. is basically a lower class phenomina
    b. is primarily gang oriented
    c. is usually related to violent incidences
    d. is found in all types of communities and neighborhoods

11. The major explanation for the rise in female criminality appears to be:
    a. based on emotional disturbances
    b. amoral in nature
    c. sociopolitical in nature
    d. sexual in nature

12. Marxist criminology is also known as:
    a. critical criminology
    b. radical criminology
    c. conflict criminology
    d. both and a b

13. Of the following, which one is <u>not</u> one of Merton's resulting behaviors in his model of goals and means:
    a. conformity
    b. ritualism
    c. complacency
    d. rebellion

14. Gangs that engage in warfare to protect their turf and provide a sense of support for their members are called:
    a. criminal gangs
    b. conflict gangs
    c. retreatist gangs
    d. rebellion gangs

15. Which criminologist is associated with the theory of differential association:
    a. Walter Miller
    b. Edwin Sutherland
    c. Emile Durkheim
    d. Albert Cohen

Matching

1. Cesare Beccaria
2. Cesare Lombroso
3. Emile Durkheim
4. Robert Merton
5. Albert Cohen
6. Walter Miller

A. Used the term "anomie" to mean absence of rules and social norms, or lawless or weakened norms, of any person or group, which may lead an individual to lose his ability to distinguish between right and wrong.

B. Maintains that criminal activities common in working-class ghetto areas because of the unique value structure that prevails there.

C. Proposed that the active criminal is a physical, biological throwback to early human evolution, who, due to his poor adjustment to the society of modern man, finds himself thrust into criminal activites.

D. Believed that laws should serve the people, protect them from governmental interference, and improve their lives.

E. Most lower class youths are unable to cope with the pressures of middle class society.

F. Argued that societies are made up of subcultures which have their own particular set of values, goals, and rules (norms) which may be in conflict with those held by members of society's predominant culture.

ESSAY QUESTIONS

1. Why isn't the deterrent power of punishment in America effective; what steps can be taken to improve effectiveness?

2. Differential Association is the best-known American theory of adult criminality; discuss the major premises of the theory and why it is or is not valid.

3. Sociobiological theories of criminality are making a comeback; explain why.

4. How important and valid do you feel conflict theories are in explaining criminality.

5. Is female criminality increasing at significant levels; give several specific reasons for your response.

CHAPTER 2 ANSWER SECTION

FILL-IN REVIEW

1. scientific, crime
2. Probability, population
3. Participant, criminologist
4. classical
5. penalties, criminal
6. Incapacitation, long
7. determined
8. biological, environment, learning
9. psychoanalytic, behavioral, cognivite, physiological
10. Anomie
11. "subculture"
12. value
13. Social process, sociocultural
14. differential association, learning
15. conventional, "drifting"
16. home, school
17. labeling, deviant
18. Conflict, controlling
19. Marxist, enterprise
20. female's
21. delinquency
22. drugs, alcohol

SELF-TEST

True-False

1. True
2. False
3. True
4. False
5. False
6. False
7. False
8. False
9. True
10. True
11. True
12. False
13. True
14. False
15. True
16. True
17. True
18. False
19. True

Multiple Choice

1. (c) Emile Durkheim
2. (a) survey research
3. (d) all of the above limit the effectiveness of general deterrence
4. (d) Cesare Lombroso
5. (b) special deterrence
6. (b) physiological
7. (a) opportunity theory
8. (d) appeal
9. (c) "getting caught"
10. (d) is found in all types of communities and neighborhoods
11. (c) sociopolitical in nature
12. (c) both a and b
13. (c) complacency
14. (b) conflict gangs
15. (b) Edwin Sutherland

Matching

1. D
2. C
3. A
4. F
5. E
6. B

CHAPTER THREE

CRIMINAL LAW

KEY TERMS AND CONCEPTS

Common Law
Law of Precedent
Stare Decisis
Substantive Law
Procedural Law
Model Penal Code
Durham Rule
M'Naghten Rule
Insanity
Intent
Male Prohibitum
Mala in se
Entrapment
Double Jeopardy
Corpus Delecti
Incapacity

Misdemeanor
Mens Rea
Criminal Negligence
Felony
Tort
Common Law
Crime
Actus Reus
Self-Defense
Civil Law
General Intent
Specific Intent
Transferred Intent
Irresistible Impulse Test
Substantial Capacity Test
Jurisdiction
Guilty but Insane

FILL-IN REVIEW

1. British law was the basis for what is known today as ____________ law.

2. The foundations of law generally can be found in ____________ decisions and ____________.

3. The ____________ criminal law defines what types of conduct are criminal and prescribes the penalties to be imposed for engaging in criminal conduct.

4. ____________ law involves the use of rules designed to implement the substantive law.

5. In ____________ law, the major concern is that the injured party be ____________ for any harm done to them.

6. In criminal law, emphasis is on the ____________ of the individual committing the crime, whereas civil law concentrates on negotiating a suitable settlement.

7. ____________ ____________ ____________ crimes are those which appear inherently wrong or evil by their nature.

8. ____________ ____________ offenses are those which are sanctioned because they are prohibited by statute.

9. The classification of crime which is most common in the United States is the ____________ -- ____________ classification; this distinction is based primarily on the degree of ____________ of the crime.

10. The term ____________ ____________ is used to describe all of the elements which together constitute a crime.

11. Mens rea conditions differ among the types of crime in terms of whether a ____________ or ____________ intent to commit the crime exists.

12. The M'Naghten Rule is also known as the ____________ test.

13. The ____________ ____________ test excuses people from criminal responsibility when they might be able to distinguish between right and wrong, but their mental condition impairs their ability to control themselves.

14. The Model Penal Code states that the test for criminal insanity is when a person lacks ____________ ____________ to know the difference between right and wrong.

15. In common law, there is generally a conclusive presumption of ____________ for a child under ____________ years of age.

16. Mens rea is that element of the crime that deals with the defendant's ____________ to commit the act, or criminal ____________ of ____________.

17. An individual can commit a crime and still be justified or excused based upon grounds of ____________ and ____________ policy.

18. The validity of any consent defense in criminal law must be based on ____________.

19. In general, individuals defending themselves from attack may use only such force as is ____________ ____________ to prevent harm.

20. The ____________ view of entrapment means that the predisposition of the defendant to commit the offense is the ____________ factor.

SELF-TEST

True-False

1. The state supreme court has the final say on whether a judicial, agency or statutory law violates the Constitution.

2. Any law in the United States, regardless of its source, must always stand the test of constitutionality.

3. Substantive law is that part of the criminal law concerned with the rules of conduct imposed by society to control antisocial behavior.

4. A crime can only result from the commission in violation of the law, and not from a failure to act.

5. Torts is another name for private wrongs, and it is part of the civil law.

6. A felony can be distinguished from a misdemeanor in that the latter is punishable by fine or imprisonment rather than by serving time in a penitentiary.

7. The in-presence requirement makes it necessary for a police officer to be present, when either a felony or misdemeanor has been committed, in order to make an arrest.

8. There are specific statutes against organized crime.

9. A crime may still be committed even though there is no concurrence of act and intent.

10. According to the doctrine of transferred intent, it is possible for an individual to be held criminally responsible for shooting one person, while meaning to shoot another.

11. The Durham Rule basically states than an accused is not criminally responsible if his unlawful act was the product of mental disease or defect.

12. Voluntary intoxication can never mitigate the degree of a crime.

13. Entrapment is a constitutional defense that protects citizens from overzealous police activity.

14. Due to the double jeopardy clause of the Constitution, a state may not re-try a defendant if his first trial ended in a hung-jury.

15. Criminal negligence differs from ordinary negligence in that it amounts to "wanton and reckless" conduct.

Multiple Choice

1. When a decision is made by a court, that decision is generally binding in similar courts in subsequent applicable cases. This is known as:
   a. stare decisis
   b. law of precedent
   c. procedural law
   d. both a and b

2. Which of the following is not a similarity between criminal and civil law:
   a. both seek to control behavior
   b. both impose sanctions
   c. both place emphasis on the intent of the individual committing the crime
   d. all of the above

3. Of the following, which act would not be considered as a mala in se crime:
   a. vagrancy
   b. robbery
   c. rape
   d. larceny/theft

4. The basic elements required to constitute a crime are known as the:
   a. actus reus
   b. mens rea
   c. corpus delecti
   d. intent

5. Criminal statutes that do not require the proof of criminal intent, or mens rea, are:
   a. private welfare crimes
   b. strict liability crimes
   c. mala in se crimes
   d. both a and b above

6. Another name for the Durham Rule is known as the:
   a. product test
   b. right-wrong test
   c. substantial capacity test
   d. impulse test

7. Consent is not an appropriate defense for:
   a. larceny/theft
   b. common law rape
   c. assaults
   d. none of the above

8. At present, the current federal laws organized into Title 18 of the U.S. Code, do not have provisions for:
   a. counterfeiting
   b. computer crimes
   c. theft
   d. forgery

9. The American Law Institute's Model Penal Code was formulated in:
   a. 1956
   b. 1960
   c. 1964
   d. 1970

10. According to the authors, the future direction of criminal law will place more attention on:
   a. white-collar crimes
   b. use of drugs
   c. traffic violations
   d. both a and b

11. The primary test for criminal responsibility in the United States is:
   a. M'Naghten Rule
   b. Irresistible Impulse Test
   c. Substantial Capacity Test
   d. Durham Rule

12. The criminal justice system is basically a ____________ system.
   a. legal
   b. political
   c. economic
   d. punishment

13. Which of the following criticisms has <u>not</u> been applied to the insanity defense:
   a. it releases criminal offenders
   b. it requires extensive use of expert testimony
   c. it spurs crime
   d. all of the above criticisms have been applied to the insanity defense

14. The corpus delecti includes:
   a. the actus reus
   b. the mens rea
   c. the combination of actus reas and mens rea
   d. all of the above

Matching

1. Mala in se
2. Mala prohibitum
3. Mens rea
4. Corpus delecti
5. Actus reus
6. General intent

A. The body of any crime.

B. To act purposely.

C. Crimes which appear inherently wrong or evil by their nature.

D. Commission of the act.

E. "The mind of the actor".

F. Offenses which are prohibited by statute.

ESSAY QUESTIONS

1. Distinguish between substantive and procedural criminal law.

2. Distinguish what constitutes the corpus delecti of a crime.

3. Compare and contract criminal and tort law. Which would you rather be tried under and why?

4. Briefly discuss the five major types of criminal defenses regarding justification or excuse; do you agree or disagree with each defense?

5. Discuss which of the different tests for criminal responsibility involving insanity you feel is the most appropriate; is there a need for a new verdict of guilty but insane?

CHAPTER 3 ANSWER SECTION

FILL-IN REVIEW

1. common
2. case, legislation
3. substantive
4. Procedural
5. civil, compensated
6. intent
7. Mala in se
8. Mala prohibitum
9. felony--misdemeanor, seriousness
10. corpus delecti
11. general, specific
12. right-wrong
13. irresistible impulse
14. substantial capacity
15. incapacity, seven
16. intent, state of mind
17. fairness, public
18. voluntariness
19. reasonably necessary
20. subjective, determining

SELF-TEST

True-False

1. False
2. True
3. True
4. False
5. True
6. True
7. False
8. False
9. False
10. True
11. True
12. False
13. False
14. False
15. True

Multiple Choice

1. (d) both a and b
2. (c) both place emphasis on the intent of the individual committing the crime
3. (a) vagrancy
4. (c) corpus delecti
5. (b) strict liability crimes
6. (a) product test
7. (c) assaults
8. (b) computer crimes
9. (c) 1964
10. (a) white-collar crimes
11. (a) M'Naghten Rule
12. (a) legal
13. (d) all of the above criticisms have been applied to the insanity defense
14. (d) all of the above

Matching

1. C
2. F
3. E
4. A
5. D
6. B

CHAPTER FOUR

AN OVERVIEW OF CRIMINAL JUSTICE

KEY TERMS AND CONCEPTS

Supreme Courts
Prosecutor
Defense Attorney
Probation
Confinement
Retribution
Deterrence
Incapacitation
Prevention
Due Process
Overcriminalization
President's Commission on Law Enforcement and Administration of Justice
National Advisory Commission on Criminal Justice Standards and Goals
Systems Models
Process Models
Organizational Models
Parole
Police
Diversion
Rehabilitation
Jail
Penitentiary
Community Based Corrections
Decriminalization
Sandra Day O'Connor
Herbert Packer
Probation
LEAA
Safe Streets Act
NCCD
ABA
Victimology

FILL-IN REVIEW

1. Criminal justice is a field of study which deals with the nature of ____________ in society, as well as an analysis of the formal processes and social ____________ which have been established for crime control.

2. The basic structure of the American criminal justice system is found in the ____________, ____________ and ____________ branches of government.

3. ___________ and ___________ constitutions grant authority for legislatures to enact and pass laws.

4. The ___________ approach to criminal justice sees a change in one element of the system as effecting change in the others.

5. The three major components of the criminal justice system in the United States are the ___________, the ___________, and ___________.

6. The two central concerns of law enforcement officers are to maintain ___________, and ___________ the criminal law.

7. Police officers today are required to exercise a great deal of individual ___________ in their roles.

8. A defendant has the right to be given due process, or to be treated with ___________ ___________.

9. The prosecutor and defense attorney are the ___________ in that aspect of the administration of criminal justice known as the ___________ system.

10. The two major functions of the defense attorney are to protect the ___________ ___________ of the accused, and give the best possible legal defense.

11. Corrections has the multi-purpose of protecting ___________, deterring ___________, and the equally important responsibility of ___________ offenders.

12. ___________ is a legal disposition allowing the offender to remain in the community subject to conditions, and under the supervision of a ___________ officer.

13. Probation officers perform the dual functions of preparing _____-_____ reports for the court, and ___________ probationers.

14. The jail is ordinarily operated by local government and is referred to as a ___________ facility.

15. Most new inmates begin their correctional experience by being sent to a ___________ and ___________ center.

16. In community-based correctional institutions, the trend is to deemphasize using large prisons and emphasize smaller, ___________ based facilities.

17. The main idea of parole is to bridge the gap between institutional ___________ and a positive ___________ within the community.

18. Criminal justice refers to a ___________ as well as to a system of agencies and organizations.

19. The removal of certain offenses from the criminal statutes represents the theory of ___________, while ___________ involves the misuse of the criminal sanction.

20. In order for a state to be eligible for LEAA funds, it must have a State Criminal Justice ___________ Agency (SPA), as required by the Safe Streets Act.

21. ___________ can be described as that area of study in the field of ___________, which is concerned with the victim of a criminal incident.

22. In the ___________ model, emphasis is on the offender and the various sequential ___________ through which he passes.

23. The ___________ model of criminal justice emphasizes roles, functions, skills, etc., and argues for a clear definition of managerial roles in criminal justice.

24. Newman's model, entitled ___________ ___________, would provide a method for previewing the entire system, emphasizing ___________ - ___________ and the flow of the criminal process.

SELF-TEST

True-False

1. The Safe Streets and Crime Control Act provides for the expenditure of federal funds for state and local crime control efforts.

2. Only recently have lawyers become active participants in seeking to improve the entire criminal justice system.

3. The basic function of the legislative system seems to be the enactment of procedural requirements.

4. The corrections component of the criminal justice system begins to function once sentencing is completed by the court.

5. All states have a standardized court structure.

6. State supreme courts may conduct criminal trials in serious cases.

7. The position of district attorney or prosecuting attorney is always an elective office.

8. The prosecutor , like the police officer, exercises a great deal of discretion in handling cases.

9. The correctional system has a relatively good performance record.

10. The origins of probation can be found in English common law.

11. Where a trial is required in the lower courts, it often occurs before a judge rather than before a jury.

12. There does not appear to be any clearly established solutions to crime control.

13. The Burger Court has taken a stricter constructionist interpretation of the Constitution than the Warren Court.

14. The authors suggest that the courts are probably least receptive to the idea of a unified system.

15. Skoler has proposed the formation of a "suger agency" to administer the criminal justice system.

16. Implicit in model building is the realization that changes in the criminal justice system are based on such models.

17. The systems model perceives criminal justice as a series of decision-making points.

18. It appears that future federal policies on crime control will adhere to the principle of improving anticrime efforts without spending more money on it.

Multiple Choice

1. The majority of criminal procedures are established by the:
   a. legislature
   b. appellate courts
   c. executive branch
   d. trial courts

2. Criminal justice agencies are created by:
   a. legislative acts
   b. executive orders
   c. constitutional requirements
   d. all of the above

3. Of the following, which criminal procedure would a Supreme Court be unlikely to perform:
   a. set bail
   b. hear felony trials
   c. review lower court decisions
   d. accept guilty pleas

4. A defendant has the right to be treated with "fundamental fairness"; this concept includes which of the following:
   a. right to be present at trial
   b. notified of the charge(s)
   c. opportunity to confront hostile witnesses
   d. all of the above

5. When an offender is sentenced by the court to a period of confinement, responsibility for custody and rehabilitation lies with the:
   a. court
   b. correction agency
   c. district attorney
   d. none of the above

6. The predominant form of release for prison inmates is:
   a. parole
   b. probation
   c. mandatory release
   d. pardon

7. A major categorical goal of the criminal justice system is the development of theoretical or abstract goals, which include:
   a. retribution and deterrence
   b. incapacitation and rehabilitation
   c. crime prevention
   d. both a and b

8. The National Advisory Commission on Criminal Justice Standards and Goals provides four priorities for reducing such offenses as homicide and robbery; which of the following was <u>not</u> one of those priorities:
   a. preventing juvenile delinquency
   b. improve social service
   c. reduction of delays in the criminal justice system
   d. all are listed priorities

9. Building stronger family units, providing counseling in schools, and developing better environmental conditions are all examples of:
   a. diversion
   b. prevention
   c. parole
   d. none of the above

10. Approximately ____________ states have enacted crime victim compensation programs:
    a. 5
    b. 10
    c. 25
    d. 40

11. The elimination of certain criminal offenses from the criminal law is called:
    a. overcriminalization
    b. undercriminalization
    c. noncriminalization
    d. decriminalization

12. The idea that an offender deserves to be punished if he or she breaks societal norms is known as:
    a. deterrence
    b. incapacitation
    c. retribution
    d. rehabilitation

13. One of the initial criticisms of LEAA was that __________ agencies were getting the largest share of funds.
    a. correctional
    b. police
    c. judicial
    d. juvenile

14. The __________ model describes the administration of criminal justice as an interrelated system of agencies, beginning with arrest and ending with release.
    a. process
    b. systems
    c. organizational
    d. managerial

15. Herpert Packer described two models which illustrate the problems of ideology in criminal justice: the crime control model and the:
    a. battle model
    b. adversary model
    c. due process model
    d. social model

16. The process model which represents the English system of criminal procedure more than the American system is the:
    a. battle model
    b. family model
    c. inquisitorial model
    d. adversary model

17. On the average, for every 500 serious crimes reported, a ratio of 1 in __________ offenders are actually sent to jail.
    a. 10
    b. 20
    c. 50
    d. 100

Matching

1. Recidivism
2. Retribution
3. Deterrence
4. Incapacitation
5. Rehabilitation

A. The view that threat of punishment will keep others from committing crime.

B. The view that an individual is responsible for his or her actions and deserves to be punished if he or she breaks societal norm.

C. The view that physical restraint will keep the offender from committing another crime.

D. The view that the offender as an individual is in need of treatment.

E. The view that many offenders return to crime after release from incarceration.

ESSAY QUESTIONS

1. List and briefly discuss the functions of the major component parts of the criminal justice system.

2. Compare and contrast the "system" of criminal justice and the "process" of criminal justice.

3. Explain the similarities and differences in parole and probation.

4. Compare and contrast the following terms: retribution, incapacitation, and rehabilitation.

5. Explain what is meant by the term "criminal justice non-system".

CHAPTER 4 ANSWER SECTION

FILL-IN REVIEW

1. crime, agencies
2. legislative, judicial, executive
3. Federal, state
4. systems
5. police, courts, corrections
6. order, enforce
7. discretion
8. fundamental fairness
9. opponents, adversary
10. constitutional rights
11. society, crime, rehabilitating
12. Probation, probation
13. pre-sentence, supervising
14. detention
15. reception, classification
16. community
17. confinement, adjustment
18. process
19. decriminalization, overcriminalization
20. Planning
21. Victimology, criminology
22. process, stages
23. management
24. functional analysis, decision-making

True-False

1. True
2. False
3 True
4. True
5. True
6. False
7. False
8. True
9. False
10. True
11. False
12. True
13. False
14. True
15. True
16. True
17. False
18. True

Multiple Choice

1. (b) appellate courts
2. (d) all of the above
3. (a) set bail
4. (d) all of the above
5. (b) correction agency
6. (a) parole
7. (d) both a and b
8. (d) all are listed priorities
9. (b) prevention
10. (d) 25
11. (d) decriminalization
12. (c) retribution
13. (b) police
14. (a) process
15. (c) due process model
16. (c) inquisitorial model
17. (b) 20

Matching

1. E
2. B
3. A
4. C
5. D

CHAPTER FIVE

THE CONSTITUTIONAL RIGHTS OF THE ACCUSED

KEY TERMS AND CONCEPTS

Bill of Rights
First Amendment
Fourth Amendment
Self-Incrimination
Privacy
Exclusionary Rule
Weeks v. United States
Incorporation
Sixth Amendment
Freedom of Speech
Search and Seizure
Selective Incorporation
Wolf v. Colorado
Eighth Amendment
Writ of Certorari
Bail
Due Process
Fourteenth Amendment
Nebraska Press Association v. Stuart
Miranda v. Arizona
Barron v. Baltimore
Palko v. Connecticut
Mapp v. Ohio
Fundamental Fairness
Separation of Powers
Cruel and Unusual Punishment

FILL-IN REVIEW

1. The ___________ of ___________, adopted by the Continental Congress in 1781, was the forerunner of our present federal Constitution.

2. The original structure of the Constitution consisted of a ___________ and ___________ articles.

3. The Bill of Rights was adopted to protect the liberties of the people from the ___________ government, and did not apply to ___________ or ___________ officials.

4. The Fourth Amendment is designed to protect the individual's right to ____________.

5. A good deal of intricate and complex legal decisions known as the law of ____________ and seizure deals with individual rights guaranteed under the ____________ amendment.

6. One of the primary purposes of the ____________ Amendment is that is provides that no person shall be compelled to be a ____________ against himself.

7. The defendant's right to a ____________ trial protects him from a secret or closed trial by making such trials unconstitutional.

8. The ____________ Amendment is interpreted to mean that a defendant must be given a jury trial where imprisonment for more than ____________ ____________ may be authorized.

9. ____________ is a money bond put up by the accused or an agent of the accused, in order to attain ____________ while awaiting trial.

10. The ____________ Amendment does not guarantee a constitutional right to bail, but rather prohibits the use of ____________ bail; the second section of this Amendment deals with "____________ and ____________ punishment".

11. The ____________ Amendment's ____________ ____________ clause applies to state government; it has been used to provide the basic liberties under the ____________ of ____________.

12. Basically, ____________ ____________ is intended to guarantee that fundamental fairness exists in each individual case.

13. There are two methods to reach the U.S. Supreme Court; the writ of ____________ being the predominant one, and the absolute right to ____________.

14. The most widely recognized theory of constitutional responsibility is entitled ____________ ____________.

15. The legal theory of ____________ ____________ became the method whereby the states were held to the same standard of criminal due process as the ____________ government.

16. The ____________ ____________ is a meeting to discuss the case and vote to reach a decision.

17. When a case is decided in the Supreme Court, the ____________ ____________ assigns someone of the majority group to write the ____________.

18. The ____________ rule states that all evidence obtained through illegal searches and ____________ is inadmissible in criminal trials.

19. In 1914 the U.S. Supreme Court decided the case of ___________ v. ___________ and barred for the first time the use of evidence obtained through an ___________ search and seizure in a ___________ prosecution.

20. The U.S. Supreme Court ___________ itself from prior decisions such as Wolf, and made the exclusionary rule applicable to state courts in the decision of ___________ vs. ___________.

21. In Mapp v. Ohio the Court re-emphasized that a relationship exists between the ___________ and ___________ Amendments forming a ___________ basis requiring exclusionary rule usage.

22. The most frequently discussed proposed limitation to the exclusionary rule is known as the "___________ ___________" exception.

SELF-TEST

True-False

1. The Nebraska Press Association v. Stuart decision dealt with the fair trial-free press issue.

2. Incorporation theory relates to the provisions of the Bill of Rights as incorporated into the Eighth Amendment's due process clause.

3. The due process clause of the Constitution only affects the procedural area of criminal law.

4. The Eighth Amendment guarantees a constitutional right to bail.

5. There are approximately 2,000 cases filed with the U.S. Supreme Court each term.

6. The Bill of Rights was adopted primarily to protect the personal liberties of individuals from state government.

7. Recent research has indicated that the Miranda v. Arizona decision has had little or no effect on either the number of confessions obtained by the police or the rate of convictions.

8. The Fourth Amendment is designed to protect the individual's right to privacy.

9. The Fifth Amendment guarantees the defendant the right to a speedy and public trial by an impartial jury.

10. The idea of "total incorporation" has never received majority support in any Supreme Court decision dealing with the Fourteenth Amendment.

11. Basically, due process is intended to insure "fundamental fairness" to each individual.

12. Selective incorporation applies to the states through the due process clause of the Fourteenth Amendment, but on a case-by-case basis only.

13. The exclusionary rule provides that all evidence obtained by searches and seizures in violation of the Sixth Amendment is inadmissible in a criminal trial.

Multiple Choice

1. The United State Constitution was ratified in which year:
   a. 1778
   b. 1781
   c. 1788
   d. 1798

2. The most widely recognized theory of constitutional responsibility is entitled:
   a. fundamental fairness
   b. incorporation theory
   c. due process
   d. selective incorporation

3. The Miranda decision was based on which amendment:
   a. Fourth
   b. Fifth
   c. Eighth
   d. Fourteenth

4. An individual's right to an attorney has been extended to stages of the criminal justice process such as:
   a. arrest
   b. line-up
   c. sentencing
   d. both b and c

5. Which of the following is a legal theory that describes the relationship of the Bill of Rights to the Fourteenth Amendment:
   a. incorporation theory
   b. theory of selective incorporation
   c. fundamental fairness
   d. all of the above

6. The U.S. Supreme Court case decision that evolved into a legal theory called fundamental fairness was:
   a. <u>Pointer</u> <u>v.</u> <u>Texas</u>
   b. <u>Palko</u> <u>v.</u> <u>Connecticut</u>
   c. <u>Malloy</u> <u>v.</u> <u>Hogan</u>
   d. none of the above

7. There are ___________ Justices on the U.S. Supreme Court.
   a. seven
   b. eight
   c. nine
   d. ten

8. The only criteria for admissibility of evidence prior to the exclusionary rule was:
   a. how it was obtained
   b. its relevancy
   c. the incriminating nature of the evidence
   d. both b and c

9. Which of the following Supreme Court decisions established the Exclusionary Rule:
   a. <u>Mapp v. Ohio</u>
   b. <u>Weeks v. United States</u>
   c. <u>Wolf v. Colorado</u>
   d. none of the above

10. <u>Mapp v. Ohio</u>, a landmark Supreme Court decision, held that:
   a. the first ten amendments were not applicable to the states.
   b. city police could not search without a warrant.
   c. if a police search was unreasonable, the evidence seized could not be used against the defendant in court.
   d. the defendant had the right, at his trial, to be confronted by the witnesses against him.

11. Which of the following events resulted in a significant change in the initial interpretation of the Constitution and the first ten amendments:
   a. <u>Barron v. Baltimore</u>
   b. <u>Hurtado v. California</u>
   c. Fourteenth Amendment
   d. both a and b

12. The Constitutional Amendment which protects the right to a speedy trial is the:
   a. First
   b. Fourth
   c. Fifth
   d. Sixth

13. By 1961, approximately ___________ of the states had adopted the Exclusionary Rule.
   a. one-fourth
   b. one-third
   c. one-half
   d. three-fourths

14. Of all the civilized countries in the world, only the ___________ applies an exclusionary rule to illegal searches and seizures of material evidence:
    a. United States
    b. Soviet Union
    c. East Germany
    d. Poland

Matching

1.	First Amendment	A.	Protects against unreasonable searches and seizures.
2.	Fourth Amendment	B.	Protects freedom of speech.
3.	Fifth Amendment	C.	Makes constitutional restrictions applicable to the states.
4.	Eighth Amendment	D.	Protects against self-incrimination.
5.	Fourteenth Amendment	E.	Protects against cruel and unusual punishment.

ESSAY QUESTIONS

1. What is the Bill of Rights and why was it added to the original Constitution?

2. Why was the Fourteenth Amendment added to the Constitution and what was its purpose?

3. What is the theory of selective incorporation?

4. What was the significance of the Supreme Court decision in *Mapp v. Ohio*?

5. Discuss why we should or should not continue to use the exclusionary rule in the United States.

CHAPTER 6 ANSWER SECTION

FILL-IN REVIEW

1. Articles of Confederation
2. preamble, seven
3. national, state, local
4. privacy
5. search, Fourth
6. Fifth, witness
7. public
8. Sixth, six months
9. Bail, freedom
10. Eighth, excessive, "cruel and Unusual"
11. Fourteenth, due process, Bill of Rights
12. due process
13. certiorari, appeal
14. selective incorporation
15. fundamental fairness, federal
16. case conference
17. Chief Justice, opinion
18. exclusionary, seizures
19. *Weeks v. United States*, illegal, federal
20. reversed, *Mapp v. Ohio*
21. Fourth and Fifth, constitutional
22. "good faith"

SELF-TEST

True-False

1. True
2. False
3. False
4. False
5. False
6. True
7. True
8. True
9. False
10. True
11. True
12. True
13. False

Multiple Choice

1. (c) 1788
2. (d) selective incorporation
3. (b) Fifth
4. (d) both b and c
5. (d) all of the above
6. (b) *Palko v. Connecticut*
7. (c) nine
8. (d) both b and c
9. (b) *Weeks v. United States*
10. (c) if a police search was unreasonable, the evidence seized could not be used against the defendant in court
11. (c) Fourteenth Amendment
12. (d) Sixth
13. (c) one-half
14. (a) United States

Matching

1. B
2. A
3. D
4. E
5. C

CHAPTER SIX

POLICE ROLES AND ORGANIZATION

KEY TERMS AND CONCEPTS

Constable
Tithing
Hundred
Shires
Shire-reeve
Watch System
Sir Robert Peel
Wilkersham Commission
August Vollmer
O. W. Wilson
IACP
LEEP
Metropolitan Police
Sheriff
State Police
Department of Justice
Federal Bureau of Investigation
NCIC
Drug Enforcement Administration
Treasury Department
Bureau of Alcohol, Tabacco, and Firearms
Internal Revenue Service
Detective Bureau
Kansas City Study
Team Policing
Basic Car Plan
Foot Patrol
Vice Squad
Selective Enforcement
Internal Affairs
Solvability Methods
Probability Methods
Police Productivity

FILL-IN REVIEW

1. In early England, people were grouped in a collective of 10 families, called a ___________, and entrusted with ___________ their own minor problems.

2. Ten tithings were grouped into a ___________, whose officers were supervised by a ___________ appointed by the local nobleman.

3. In the thirteenth century, during the reign of King ___________ , the ___________ system was created to help protect property in England's larger cities and towns.

4. The first organized police force was established in London in the year ___________ by Sir ___________ ___________.

5. ___________ created the first formal U.S. police department in 1838; the new departments replaced the ___________ system.

6. Police during the nineteenth century were generally incompetent, ___________, and disliked by the people they served.

7. The ___________ Commission was created by President Hoover to study police issues on a ___________ scale.

8. While serving as police chief of Berkeley, California, ___________ instituted ___________ training as an important part of his development of young officers.

9. During the 1960's the ___________ ___________ movement produced a growing tension between black citizens who were demanding increased rights and freedoms, and the police, whose role often became focused on security and maintaining the ___________ ___________.

10. The 1970's saw increased recruitment of ___________ and ___________ police officers.

11. There is now agreement among police experts that police forces should be evaluated not on their ___________ ability but on their courteousness, deportment, and helpfulness.

12. There are approximately ___________ law enforcement agencies in the United States.

13. Most of the nation's county police departments are independent agencies whose senior officer, the ___________, is usually an ___________ political official.

14. The Federal Bureau of Investigation is not a police agency but an ___________ agency, which limits its jurisdictions to Federal ___________ not specifically assigned to other agencies.

15. The ___________ ___________ is an arm of the Treasury Department, and was ofiginally charged with enforcing laws against counterfeiting.

16. Research conducted in the 1960's and 1970's showed that the great bulk of a patrol officer's time is spent on ___________ ___________ or peacekeeping and not on ___________ ___________ duties.

17. The ___________ ___________ study indicated that variations in preventive patrol tactics, from proactive to ___________, had little effect on the ___________ patterns in the separate locales.

18. The Police Foundation study on foot patrol showed that while it did not influence the crime rate, residents perceived greater ___________ safety and were less afraid of crime.

19. The purpose of ___________ ___________ is to create strong ties between police officers and the community they serve and to involve the neighborhood in police ___________.

20. The Rand researchers estimated that ___________ of all detectives could be replaced without negatively influeing crime ___________ rates.

21. A branch of a larger police department which is charged with "policing the police" is known as ___________ ___________.

22. O. W. ___________ classic text, Police ___________, became the basic tool with which police administrators attempted to improve their department's management.

23. A recent survey of changes in police selection practices found that there was a trend toward relating ___________ requirements and an increased use of ___________ and ___________ test measures.

SELF-TEST

True-False

1. Under the pledge system people were grouped in a collective of 10 families called a shire.

2. The watch system was created to help protect property in England's larger cities and towns.

3. Through the 1960's, police professionalism was interpreted in terms of a tough, highly trained, rule-oriented law enforcement department organized along military lines.

4. There is strong evidence that the technological and operational advantages of the 1960's and 1970's have helped improve police effectiveness in the 1980's.

5. Research conducted in the 1960's and 1970's showed that most of a patrol officer's time is spent on crime-fighting duties.

6. Selective enforcement means that police departments attempt to cite all traffic violators.

7. In general, team policing has been operationally successful in police agencies.

8. In general, physical requirements are being related to police selection practices.

9. Police productivity refers primarily to the number of arrests made by the police over a certain time period.

10. Probability computer models are "predictive in nature".

11. The concept of state control of local law enforcement agencies in America was successful because it centralized police operations.

12. One of the problems the Wickersham Commission noted in 1931 was that an average police chief's term of office was too short.

13. The duties of a county sheriff's department vary according to the size and development of the county in which it is seated.

14. The Secret Service is an arm of the U.S. Justice Department.

Multiple Choice

1. Hundreds were grouped into ____________ which resemble the counties of today.
   a. shires
   b. shire-reeves
   c. tithings
   d. both a and b

2. In what year did Sir Robert Peel establish the London police force:
   a. 1776
   b. 1796
   c. 1829
   d. 1859

3. Which of the following individuals had a significant impact on improving police administration and management.
   a. A. Vollmer
   b. O. W. Wilson
   c. W. Webster
   d. J. Edgar Hoover

4. The reason's for the turmoil and crisis the police went through in the 1960's and 1970's can be contributed to:
   a. social problems
   b. Supreme Court rulings
   c. rapidly growing crime rate
   d. all of the above

5. There are approximately ___________ law enforcement agencies in the United States.
   a. 10,000
   b. 20,000
   c. 40,000
   d. 50,000

6. The legal arm of the United States government is the:
   a. U.S. Department of Justice
   b. U.S. Treasury Department
   c. Federal Bureau of Investigation
   d. Customs Bureau

7. Which of the following does the FBI offer to aid local law enforcement agencies:
   a. NCIC
   b. Crime Laboratory
   c. UCR
   d. all of the above

8. The ___________ Act established federal jurisdiction over the supply and use of narcotics:
   a. Hobbs
   b. Mann
   c. Dyer
   d. Harrison

9. The Bureau of Alcohol, Tobacco, and Firearms falls under the ___________ Department:
   a. Justice
   b. Treasury
   c. Customs
   d. Defense

10. The major purpose(s) of patrol is to:
    a. create a feeling of security in the community
    b. maintain public order
    c. enable the police to respond quickly where needed
    d. all of the above

11. The Kansas City study indicated that variations in patrol techniques:
    a. had little effect on crime patterns
    b. had little effect on citizen attitudes toward the police
    c. both a and b
    d. none of the above

12. According to one study, approximately ___________ percent of all police departments require only a high school diploma for entry level positions:
    a. 25%
    b. 50%
    c. 65%
    d. 80%

13. The first formal police department in the United States was developed in:
    a. New York
    b. Philadelphia
    c. Baltimore
    d. Boston

14. Rand researchers estimated that ___________ of all detectives could be replaced without negatively influence crime clearance rates:
    a. 10%
    b. 25%
    c. 50%
    d. 60%

15. The Police Foundation study on foot patrol found:
    a. foot patrol did not influence the crime rate significantly
    b. foot patrol did influence the crime rate significantly
    c. foot patrol helped citizens improve their attitudes toward the efforts of police
    d. both a and c

Matching

1.	James Q. Wilson	A.	Police Administration
2.	August Vollmer	B.	Watch System
3.	Robert Peel	C.	Investigative function as four types of action
4.	Edward I	D.	Emphasized university trained police officers
5.	O. W. Wilson	E.	"Act for improving the police in and near the metropolis"

ESSAY QUESTIONS

1. Discuss the major impact of technology on police organizations and their effectiveness; what about the future?

2. What do you feel is the best measurement of police productivity and why?

3. Describe the major role or responsibilities police should concentrate on in a democratic society.

4. Discuss the possible future implications suggested by the results of the Kansas City study on preventive patrol, the Rand study on detectives and the Police Foundation study on foot patrol.

5. Briefly discuss several possible advantages/disadvantages of the team policing concept.

CHAPTER 6 ANSWER SECTION

FILL-IN REVIEW

1. tithing, policing
2. hundred, constable
3. Edward, watch
4. 1829, Robert Peel
5. Boston, nightwatch
6. corrupt
7. Wickersham, national
8. Vollmer, university
9. civil rights, status quo
10. women, minority
11. crimefighting
12. 20,000
13. sheriff, elected
14. investigative, laws
15. Secret Service
16. order maintenance, crime-fighting
17. Kansas City, reactive, crime
18. safety
19. team policing, operations
20. half, clearance
21. internal affairs
22. Wilson's, Administration
23. physical, intelligence, personality

SELF-TEST

True-False

1. False
2. True
3. True
4. False
5. False
6. False
7. False
8. True
9. False
10. True
11. False
12. True
13. True
14. False

Multiple Choice

1. (a) shires
2. (c) 1829
3. (b) O. W. Wilson
4. (d) all of the above
5. (b) 20,000
6. (a) U.S. Department of Justice
7. (d) all of the above
8. (d) Harrison
9. (b) Treasury
10. (d) all of the above
11. (c) both a and b
12. (d) 80%
13. (d) Boston
14. (c) 50%
15. (d) both a and c

Matching

1. C
2. D
3. E
4. B
5. A

CHAPTER SEVEN

ISSUES IN POLICING

KEY TERMS AND CONCEPTS

Police Brutality
Police Corruption
Police Personality
Working Personality
Field Training Officer
Police Culture
Police Officer Style
Crime Fighter
Social Agent
Law Enforcer
Watchman
Discretion
Demeanor

Sherman Report
Police*woman*
*Police*woman
Stress
Police-Community Relations
Deadly Force
Model Penal Code
Mattis v. Schnarr
Wiley v. Memphis Police Department
Knapp Commission
Meat Eaters
Grass Eaters
On the Pad

FILL-IN REVIEW

1. A national survey conducted by Louis Harris found that 79 percent of Americans believe police have little ___________ effect on ___________.

2. Research by Milton Rokeach suggests that most police officers probably had a unique value orientation and ___________ prior to beginning their careers.

3. Other researchers, such as John Van Maanen, argue that a police personality is developed through the ___________ of becoming a law enforcement officer.

4. Michael Brown argues that a police ___________ is created to meet the recurring anxiety and emotional ___________ that are part of police work.

5. The ___________ ___________ believes that police should get involved in a wide range of activities.

6. The Crime Fighter can be distinguished from the Law Enforcer in that the latter does not separate between ___________ and ___________ crimes.

7. The Watchman style places emphasis on the maintenance of public ___________ as the primary police goal.

8. The evidence shows that the police ___________ involves a preponderance of non-crime related activities.

9. Jerome Skolnick has termed the exercise of police discretion as a prime example of ___________ ___________ decision-making in criminal justice.

10. Studies have found that police officers rely heavily on ___________ in making decisions.

11. Police administrators must create a ___________ which inspires patrol officers and encourages them to exercise their discretion properly.

12. The Sherman Report is critical of police educational programs with limited ___________ orientations.

13. While the jury is still out on the value of police education, there is some indication that it does have a ___________ influence on police ___________.

14. Minorities and women tend to be ___________ in police departments.

15. In the Washington, D.C. study of policewomen, it was found that women were more likely than their male colleagues to receive ___________ from the community and were less likely to be charged with ___________ conduct.

16. Adrian Kinnane suggests that the rejection of female officers by male officers is often caused by the males' allegiance to a "___________" oriented police ___________.

17. The ___________ attempts to be more loyal, hardworking, and tough than women are generally expected to be.

18. One of the dangers of court-ordered hiring of minority officers is that white ___________ may occur.

19. The key to improving police community relations may lie in improving the ___________ and ___________ of every police officer and not the creation of specialized PCR units.

20. Nicholas Alex uses the term "___________ ___________" in reference to the black officer's dilemma of expectations to give members of his own race a break, and overt racism from his police colleagues.

21. Reiss found that ___________ abuse of citizens by police is quite common; conversely, excessive use of ___________ force is relatively rare.

22. The justification for the use of deadly force can be traced to English ___________ ___________, in which almost every criminal offense merited a felony status and subsequent ___________ ___________.

23. The Model Penal Code rule on deadly force suggests the police evaluate the danger to the ___________, the ___________, and ___________ as a whole before any action can justify the use of violence by police.

24. The case of Mattis v. ___________ is one of the few cases in which a court overruled a police ___________ policy.

25. The Knapp Commission classified corruption among police officers into two categories: "___________ ___________" and "___________ ___________".

SELF-TEST

True-False

1. Most police officers band together in a "police subculture" characterized by clannishness, secrecy, and insulation from others in society.

2. No single explanation has satisfactorily accounted for the various forms the abuse of police power takes.

3. Researchers have generally concluded that a unique police personality does not exist.

4. It has been found that an offender's demeanor can significantly influence police discretion.

5. The development of higher education for police officers has been recommended by national commissions on policing since 1931.

6. The Sherman Report is generally favorable of current police education practices.

7. College educated police officers tend to receive fewer citizen complaints.

8. The enforcement "style" employed by a police officer generally has a large impact on the amount of discretion he employs.

9. Arthur Niederhoffer found that police cynicism increases with the length of service.

10. Studies show that women officers perform just as well with male as with female officers.

11. Most evidence suggests that a police personality is developed through the on-going process of doing police work.

12. One national survey found that approximately 80 percent of Americans believe the police have little deterrent effect on crime.

13. Meat eaters accept payoffs when their everyday duties place them in a position to be solicited by the public.

14. In reality, police officer's crime-fighting efforts are only a small part of their overall activities.

15. The common law standard of allowing police use of deadly force when apprehending a fleeing felon is not in practice today.

Multiple Choice

1. The style of policing in which the officer considers himself to be a problem-solver is:
   a. watchman
   b. social agent
   c. crime fighter
   d. law enforcer

2. The strategy of maintaining a low profile and intervening only when there is a clear indication of public danger is that of a:
   a. crime fighter
   b. social agent
   c. watchman
   d. law enforcer

3. According to a research study conducted by Webster, police spend about half their time on:
   a. administrative functions
   b. travel and surveillance
   c. criminal investigations
   d. social service functions

4. Which of the following is <u>not</u> an environmental influence on police discretion:
   a. policies, practices, and customs of the police department
   b. peer group pressure
   c. pressure exerted by individual supervisors on the officers.
   d. all of the above influence discretion

5. Deadly force refers to the actions of a police officer who shoots and kills a suspect:
   a. fleeing from arrest
   b. assaulting a victim
   c. attacking the police officer
   d. all of the above

6. The number of states that adhere to the common law rule of allowing police to shoot fleeing felons, even though not presenting an immediate danger, is:
   a. ten or less
   b. seventeen
   c. twenty-four
   d. over twenty-five

7. Many experts believe that the key to improving police community relations is:
   a. to improve the sensitivity and performance of police officers
   b. to create specialized PCR units
   c. to increase the number of patrol officers
   d. to decrease the number of patrol officers

8. The style of police work in which the officer is interested primarily in dealing with "hard" crimes is called the:
   a. Social Agent
   b. Crime Fighter
   c. Law Enforcer
   d. Watchman

9. Which of the following factors does <u>not</u> relate to police shootings:
   a. firearm availability
   b. social variables
   c. police workload
   d. all of the above relate to police shootings

10. Which category of police corruption involves participation by police in serious criminal behaviors:
   a. bribery and extortion
   b. active criminality
   c. selective enforcement (nonenforcement)
   d. none of the above

11. Jerome Skolnick has described the police officer's ____________ personality as being shaped by constant exposure to danger and the need to use force and authority to reduce and control threatening situations.
   a. cynical
   b. authoritarian
   c. working
   d. paranoid

12. Which of the following factors does <u>not</u> influence police discretion:
    a. departmental policies
    b. peer pressure
    c. race
    d. all of the above influence discretion

13. The Sherman Report:
    a. is critical of current police education techniques
    b. is controversial in many quarters of law enforcement education
    c. suggests that the nuts and bolts of police procedures should be stressed
    d. both a and b

14. Kinnane suggests that rejection of female officers is often caused by the males' allegiance to a ___________ oriented police culture.
    a. macho
    b. corruption
    c. racist
    d. suspicion

15. Which of the following factors does <u>not</u> relate to police stress:
    a. internal conflict with administrative policies
    b. Dirty Harry Problem
    c. role conflict
    d. both a and b

Matching

1.	Arthur Niederhoffer	A.	Police personality
2.	James Q. Wilson	B.	Police officer style
3.	Jerome Skolnick	C.	Police Culture
4.	Michael Brown	D.	Police cynacism
5.	Milton Rokeach	E.	Working personality

ESSAY QUESTIONS

1. Describe several styles of police work; which style do you think is the most appropriate for your community?

2. What is police discretion?; list several methods police departments can utilize to control such discretion.

3. Briefly discuss why police departments should attempt to hire qualified women and minority group members.

4. Describe and defend a policy you think should be used regarding deadly force.

5. Give several reasons why or why not a college degree should be a requirement to become a police officer.

CHAPTER 7 ANSWER SECTION

FILL-IN REVIEW

1. deterrent, crime
2. personality
3. experience
4. culture, stress
5. Social Agent
6. major, minor
7. order
8. role
9. low, visibility
10. demeanor
11. climate
12. academic
13. beneficial, performance
14. underrepresented
15. support, improper
16. "macho", culture
17. policewoman
18. backlash
19. sensitivity, performance
20. "double marginality"
21. verbal, physical
22. common law, death penalty
23. suspect, officer, society
24. Schnarr, shooting
25. meat eaters, grass eaters

True-False

1. True
2. True
3. False
4. True
5. True
6. False
7. True
8. False
9. True
10. True
11. True
12. True
13. False
14. True
15. False

Multiple Choice

1. (b) social agent
2. (c) watchman
3. (a) administrative functions
4. (d) all of the above influence discretion
5. (d) all of the above
6. (c) twenty-four
7. (a) to improve the sensitivity and performance of police officers
8. (b) Crime Fighter
9. (d) all of the above relate to police shootings
10. (b) active criminality
11. (c) working
12. (d) all of the above influence discretion
13. (d) both a and b
14. (a) macho
15. (b) Dirty Harry Problem

Matching

1. D
2. B
3. E
4. C
5. A

CHAPTER EIGHT

THE POLICE PROCESS

KEY TERMS AND CONCEPTS

Police Investigation
Search and Seizure
Fourth Amendment
Unreasonableness
Probable Cause
Particularity
Spinelli v. United States
Aguilar v. Texas
Chimel v. California
Stop and Frisk
Threshold Inquiry
Payton v. New York
Terry v. Ohio
Consent
United States v. Mendenhall
Chambers v. Maroney
United States v. Ross
Katz v. United States
Arrest
Miranda v. Arizona
Escabedo v. Illinois
United States v. Wade
Suggestiveness
Neil v. Biggers

FILL-IN REVIEW

1. The police become aware of a crime either through a reported ___________ or through a personal ___________.

2. Evidence collected by the police is governed by ___________ and ___________ requirements of the ___________ Amendment.

3. A ___________ ___________ is a court order authorizing and directing the police to search a designated place for ___________ stated in the order.

4. ____________ in searches and seizures generally refers to whether an officer exceeds the scope of police authority.

5. A search warrant cannot be issued but upon ____________ ____________ supported by oath or affirmation.

6. A search warrant must specify the place to be searched and the reasons for searching it; this is known as ____________.

7. The legality of a ____________ search, incident to arrest, depends almost entirely on the ____________ of the arrest.

8. With a limited ____________ and ____________ power, the police officer is able to investigate suspicious persons and situations without having to meet the ____________ ____________ standard for arrest.

9. The Supreme Court has continued to interpret the ______ v. ______ case as an exception to the general rule requiring probable cause for arrest.

10. Those who give their ____________ to search essentially ____________ their constitutional rights under the Fourth Amendment.

11. The ____________ search of an automobile is valid if the police have probable cause to believe that the car contains ____________ they are seeking.

12. To justify the use of wiretapping, the police must normally request a ____________ ____________ based upon probable cause.

13. The Omnibus Crime Control Act provides legislative controls over the interception of ____________ communication.

14. For all practical purposes, an arrest has occurred once a person has been ____________ of his or her ____________.

15. In the case of a felony, most jurisdictions provide that an officer may arrest a suspect without a warrant where probable cause exists even though the officer was not ____________ when the offense was ____________.

16. Prior to Miranda, the principal test for the admissibility of a confession or admission was whether the statements were made ____________.

17. Regarding Miranda, a suspect who comes under police custody at the time of ____________, must be warned of the right under the ____________ Amendment to be free from ______-______ prior to any questioning.

18. The Miranda warning is not required as long as the person is not in custody and the questioning is of an ____________ and ____________ nature.

19. It appears that the Supreme Court has chipped away at the *Miranda* ruling in recent years, holding that statements made in violation of it can be used for limited __________ purposes.

20. If determining the identity of a suspect is "__________" it is in violation of the due process clause of the Fifth and Fourteenth Amendments.

21. The length of station-house detention is strictly limited by __________; the police must bring the accused before the __________ as quickly as possible.

SELF-TEST

True-False

1. Unreasonableness in searches and seizures refers to whether an officer has adequately obtained a search warrant.

2. Threshold inquiry refers to stop and frisk procedures.

3. The validity of a search warrant, once issued, is determined by the information contained in the affidavit.

4. Immediate control refers to the area where a person can reach for a weapon or destroy evidence.

5. The stop and frisk procedure is a court standard, and it has not been codified through legislation.

6. The stop and frisk procedure may be used in order to conduct exploratory searches.

7. The burden rests on the state to show that a consent search was voluntarily given.

8. The police are under no obligation to inform a suspect that he can refuse his consent to a search.

9. The permissible scope of a search incident to a lawful arrest was dealt with in the *Chimel v. California* case.

10. Essentially, the same basic rules are applied to the search of a car as they are to a search of a home.

11. A police officer is not required to tell the suspect he is under arrest in order to effect an arrest.

12. A defendant has the right to counsel during a line-up, whether or not he has been formally charged with a crime.

13. In Escobedo v. Illinois, the court held that the voluntariness of a confession is based on the totality of the circumstances.

14. When the right to counsel is violated, the evidence of any pretrial identification must be excluded from the trial.

15. Basically, the Miranda warning must be given anytime a suspect is to be questioned.

Multiple Choice

1. Evidence from a police informer is normally referred to as:
   a. second-hand evidence
   b. testimonial evidence
   c. hearsay evidence
   d. sworn evidence

2. A two-part credibility test of hearsay evidence obtained from informants can be found in the case of:
   a. Spinelli v. United States
   b. Aguilar v. Texas
   c. Chimel v. California
   d. Terry v. Ohio

3. A warrantless arrest for a felony requires:
   a. probable cause
   b. the officer's presence at the time of the crime
   c. both a and b
   d. none of the above

4. An exception to the rule requiring a search is the field interrogation known as:
   a. stop and frisk
   b. threshold inquiry
   c. safety exception
   d. both a and b

5. The case utilized by the Supreme Court to create the stop and frisk exception to the search warrant requirement is:
   a. Terry v. Ohio
   b. Chimel v. California
   c. Aguilar v. Texas
   d. Dunaway v. New York

6. The main legal issue in consent searches is whether the person:
   a. knew that he could refuse consent
   b. was acting suspiciously
   c. gave the consent voluntarily
   d. all of the above

7. In _Katz v. United States_, the Supreme Court concluded that a search results when the police violate a person's:
   a. home
   b. privacy
   c. legal rights
   d. person

8. The Supreme Court's ruling in ____________ changed the policy in regard to the scope of a search to the defendant and the immediate physical surroundings under the defendant's control.
   a. _Dunaway v. New York_
   b. _Katz v. United States_
   c. _Terry v. Ohio_
   d. _Chimel v. California_

9. Frisking of persons, vehicles, and premises may be initiated:
   a. in connection with arrest
   b. to acquire evidence
   c. to protect the officer
   d. all of the above

10. An arrest may be made without a warrant only where:
   a. the officer is able to show probable cause that a crime occurred, and the person being arrested committed it
   b. the law of the jurisdiction allows for arrest without a warrant
   c. both a and b
   d. none of the above

11. A warrantless arrest for a misdemeanor requires:
   a. probable cause
   b. the officer's presence at the time of the crime
   c. both a and b
   d. none of the above

12. A defendant has the right to counsel during:
   a. post-indictment line-up
   b. pretrial line-up
   c. pre-indictment line-up
   d. any form of line-up

13. For all practical purposes, a person is under arrest when:
   a. his liberty has been taken from him
   b. a police officer stops him
   c. he is brought to the station house
   d. all of the above

14. In which of the following cases did the U.S. Supreme Court determine that the police must obtain a search warrant for an arrest when entering a suspect's home to make a routine felony arrest:
   a. _Katz v. United States_
   b. _Chambers v. Maroney_
   c. _Neil v. Biggers_
   d. _Payton v. New York_

15. The case of ___________ concluded that if probable cause exists to believe that an automobile contains criminal evidence, a warrantless search by police is permissible.
    a. *United States v. Ross*
    b. *Chimel v. California*
    c. *Terry v. Ohio*
    d. none of the above

Matching

1. Line-up
2. Chimel
3. Katz
4. Probable Cause
5. Mendenhall
6. Escobedo
7. Ross

A. Stop and frisk.

B. Permissible scope of a search incident to lawful arrest.

C. Voluntariness of a confession is not based on the totality of the circumstances.

D. Reason to believe.

E. A non-material invasion of privacy can constitute search.

F. Identification process.

G. Automobile searches.

ESSAY QUESTIONS

1. Discuss the four major exceptions to the search warrant requirement of the Fourth Amendment; be sure to include what constitutes legality for each situation and give at least one example of each.

2. Describe the facts, the decision, and most importantly the significance of the *Chimel v. California* case.

3. Discuss where the law stands today regarding warrantless searches of automobiles; what is the significance of the *United States v. Ross* case?

4. What is the purpose of a threshold inquiry or stop and frisk procedure?

5. Discuss the factors leading up to the *Miranda* decision and under what circumstances the warnings must be given; give several reasons why you agree or disagree with this ruling.

CHAPTER 8 ANSWER SECTION

FILL-IN REVIEW

1. complaint, investigation
2. search, seizure, Fourth
3. search warrant, property
4. Unreasonableness
5. probable cause
6. particularlity
7. warrantless, lawfulness
8. stop, frisk, probable cause
9. _Terry_ _v._ _Ohio_
10. consent, waive
11. warrantless, evidence
12. court order
13. oral
14. deprived, liberty
15. present, committed
16. voluntarily
17. arrest, Fifth, self-incrimination
18. investigative, nonaccusatory
19. trial
20. suggestive
21. law, court

SELF-TEST

True-False

1. False
2. True
3. True
4. True
5. False
6. False
7. True
8. True
9. True
10. False
11. True
12. False
13. False
14. True
15. False

Multiple Choice

1. (c) hearsay evidence
2. (b) *Aguilar v. Texas*
3. (a) probable cause
4. (d) both a and b
5. (a) *Terry v. Ohio*
6. (c) gave the consent voluntarily
7. (b) privacy
8. (d) *Chimel v. California*
9. (d) all of the above
10. (c) both a and b
11. (c) both a and b
12. (a) post-indictment line-up
13. (a) his liberty is taken from him
14. (d) *Payton v. New York*
15. (a) *United States v. Ross*

Matching

1. F
2. B
3. E
4. D
5. A
6. C
7. G

CHAPTER NINE

THE PROSECUTION AND THE DEFENSE

KEY TERMS AND CONCEPTS

Prosecutor
District Attorney
U.S. Attorney
Pretrial Motion
Indigent
Public Defender
Procedural Error
Admissibility
Adversary
Prosecutorial Discretion
Defense Attorney
Assigned Counsel System
Mixed Counsel System
House Counsel
Collateral Proceedings
United States v. Goodwin
Prosecutorial Vindictiveness Doctrine
Sixth Amendment
Gideon v. Wainwright
Gagnon v. Scarpelli
Argersinger v. Hamlin
Morrissey v. Brewer
United States v. DeCoster

FILL-IN REVIEW

1. The three major participants in the criminal trial process are the ____________, the ____________, and the ____________ ____________.

2. The prosecutor has a fundamental obligation to seek ____________ as well as to convict those who are ____________.

3. The prosecutor is either ____________ or ____________ and is consequently a political figure in the criminal justice system.

4. In the federal system, prosecutors are known as ____________ ____________ ____________ and are appointed by the ____________.

5. The key to the prosecutorial function is the power to institute formal ___________ against the ___________.

6. A majority of the prosecutor's work comes from ___________ initiated by citizens or ___________ made by the police.

7. Too much prosecutorial ___________ can lead to abuses which result in the abandonment of the law.

8. In cases involving ___________ offenses, the decision to charge a person may be left primarily to the discretion of the ___________ ___________ agency.

9. In pretrial ___________, the prosecutor postpones criminal prosecution in exchange for the defendant's participation in a ___________ program.

10. For many years, the role of the criminal ___________ attorney and the practice of criminal ___________ have generally been placed in a low status position by the legal profession and community.

11. Since most people accused of crimes cannot afford their own attorneys, the vast majority of defense work is done by the ___________ ___________ or by a private attorney appointed by the ___________ at fixed rates paid by the government.

12. To fulfill the role of the truly professional advocate, the defense lawyer must be able to conduct the case free from interference, and have complete ___________ of all the facts of the case.

13. The twin duties of a defense lawyer are to his or her ___________ and the ___________.

14. In the landmark case of Gideon v. Wainwright, the United States Supreme Court held that state courts must provide ___________ to the ___________ defendant in ___________ cases.

15. In the case of ______ v. ______, the court extended the obligation to provide counsel in all cases where the penalty includes imprisonment.

16. In the case of Gagnon v. Scarpelli, the court held that the parolee and probationer are to be provided with counsel in ___________ hearings on a case-by-case basis.

17. Programs providing assistance of counsel to indigents are organized into two major categories: ___________ defender systems and ___________ counsel systems.

18. Because there is no easy way to make prosecutorial decisions, it has been recommended that the prosecutor establish ___________ for evaluating whether criminal ___________ should be brought against the accused.

19. In major ____________ areas, the taxpayer-supported public defender system is becoming the basic type of legal ____________.

20. The case of United States v. ____________ produced some general guidelines on the meaning of "reasonable competent assistance of counsel".

SELF-TEST

True-False

1. Much of the conflict between the police and the prosecutor stems from the prosecutor's unlimited discretion whether or not to proceed with an accusation.

2. In felony cases, the prosecutor has little discretion in deciding whether to charge the accused with a crime.

3. In pretrial diversion the criminal prosecution is postponed or eliminated in exchange for the alleged offender's participation in a rehabilitation program.

4. The major duties of any defense attorney, whether privately employed, appointed by the court, or serving as public defender, are the same.

5. The chief law enforcement officer of a specific jurisdiction is the prosecutor.

6. Prosecutors are elected in the federal system, and are known as United States attorneys.

7. If an individual has not been indicated or formally charged with a crime, he is not entitled to be represented by counsel.

8. Lawyers have been reluctant to specialize in criminal law because the pay is relatively low, and they often end up providing services without receiving any compensation.

9. Indigent defendants in state courts have always been afforded an attorney.

10. A probationer has the right to counsel at a deferred sentence hearing.

11. A defendant has the right to counsel for a discretionary appellate review.

12. The right to counsel is not spelled out in any federal or state statutes.

13. The basic reason for introducing an intermediary into the defense process is to compensate for the client's inarticulateness.

14. A prosecutor is ethically obliged to present all charges that the evidence may support.

Multiple Choice

1. What defense system is most likely to suffer from inadequate legal fees and a lack of support and supervision:
   a. mixed counsel system
   b. assigned counsel method
   c. public defender system
   d. all of the above

2. The prosecutor would be unlikely to work together with a police officer in:
   a. helping to prepare the court officer for trial appearances
   b. limiting unnecessary court appearances by the officer
   c. training programs
   d. conducting line-ups for the purposes of identification

3. In the criminal trial process, who has the authority to bring the accused to trial:
   a. police
   b. prosecutor
   c. judge
   d. all of the above

4. Prosecutorial discretion is beneficial because:
   a. professional standards insure just decisions
   b. it allows for alternative procedures
   c. it serves as a screening process, eliminating many causes
   d. both b and c

5. In reference to prosecutorial practices, the definition of discretion implies the need to choose among alternative decisions such as modification of:
   a. criminal charges
   b. removal of cases from the criminal process
   c. prosecuting to the fullest extent of legal authority
   d. all of the above

6. The opportunity to deal with the accused in a noncriminal fashion represents what has become known as pretrial:
   a. discretion
   b. diversion
   c. distraction
   d. deterrence

7. Which of the following is <u>not</u> a function of the defense counsel:
   a. providing assistance at sentencing
   b. investigating the incident
   c. entering plea negotiations
   d. all of the above are functions

8. The federal court system has long-provided counsel to indigent defendants based on the __________ Amendment of the United States Constitution.
   a. Sixth
   b. Fifth
   c. Eighth
   d. Fourth

9. Which Supreme Court case took the first major step toward establishing that state courts must provide defense counsel to indigent defendants in felony prosecutions:
   a. Gideon v. Wainwright
   b. Miranda v. Arizona
   c. Argersinger v. Hamlin
   d. Morrissey v. Brewer

10. Which of the following cases decided procedural due process guidelines for parole revocation hearings:
   a. Morrissey v. Brewer
   b. Gideon v. Wainwright
   c. Hamilton v. Alabama
   d. Berger v. United States

11. At which of the following is the indigent defendant not required by Supreme Court decision to be represented by counsel:
   a. at interrogation when in custody of the police
   b. at a police line-up when formally charged with a crime
   c. at grand jury investigations
   d. at arraignment

12. The National Advisory Commission on Criminal Justice Standards and Goals has recommended that counsel be made available to the indigent defendant in all criminal cases from time of:
   a. arrest
   b. arraignment
   c. interrogation
   d. incarceration

13. Which case produced some general guidelines on the meaning of "reasonably competent assistance of counsel":
   a. United States v. Goodwin
   b. United States v. DeCoster
   c. Morrissey v. Brewer
   d. Bordenkircher v. Hayes

14. Which of the following factors have not been identified by Frank Miller as affecting the prosecutor's charging decision:
   a. the cost of the prosecution
   b. the willingness of the suspect to cooperate
   c. the attitude of the victim
   d. all of the above affect the prosecutor's charging decision

15. It is estimated that there are over __________ lawyers in America.
    a. 100,000
    b. 250,000
    c. 400,000
    d. 600,000

Matching

1. House counsel
2. <u>Hamilton v. Alabama</u>
3. <u>United States v. Goodwin</u>
4. <u>Argersinger v. Hamlin</u>
5. Pretrial diversion
6. <u>United States v. DeCoster</u>
7. <u>Gagnon v. Scarpelli</u>
8. Collateral proceedings

A. Prosecutorial vindictiveness doctrine

B. Revocation of probation, patrole, etc

C. Assistance of counsel to parolee and probationer in revocation hearings on a case-by-case basis.

D. Postponement or elimination of criminal prosecution

E. Assistance of counsel in all criminal cases where penalty includes imprisonment.

F. Defense of professional criminals.

G. Assistance of counsel must be provided at arraignments, preliminary hearings

H. Reasonably competent counsel

ESSAY QUESTIONS

1. Elaborate on Justice Sutherland's quote regarding the prosecutor's dilemma that, "the two-fold aim....is that guilt shall not escape or innocence suffer". What is the essence of this statement in relation to the prosecutor's responsibilities?

2. List some factors which the prosecutor may properly consider in exercising his discretion.

3. Why was the role of the criminal defense attorney considered to be relatively "undesirable" in the past? What recent changes have been made?

4. Why should defendants be discouraged from defending themselves? What sorts of suspicions are especially critical in this area?

5. Briefly discuss the meaning of being provided with "reasonably competent" counsel; include recent case law decisions.

CHAPTER 9 ANSWER SECTION

FILL-IN REVIEW

1. judge, prosecutor, defense attorney
2. justice, guilty
3. elected, appointed
4. United States Attorneys, President
5. charges, defendant
6. complaints, arrests
7. discretion
8. minor, law enforcement
9. diversion, rehabilitation
10. defense, law
11. public defender, court
12. disclosure
13. client, court
14. counsel, indigent, felony
15. _Argersinger_ _v._ _Hamlin_
16. revocation
17. public, assigned
18. standards, proceedings
19. metropolitan, representation
20. _DeCoster_

SELF-TEST

True-False

1. True
2. False
3. True
4. True
5. True
6. False
7. True
8. True
9. False
10. True
11. False
12. False
13. False
14. True

Multiple Choice

1. (b) assigned counsel method
2. (d) conducting line-ups for the purposes of identification
3. (b) prosecutor
4. (d) both b and c
5. (d) all of the above
6. (b) diversion
7. (d) all of the above are functions
8. (a) Sixth
9. (a) _Gideon v. Wainwright_
10. (a) _Morrissey v. Brewer_
11. (c) at grand jury investigations
12. (a) arrest
13. (b) _United States v. DeCoster_
14. (d) all of the above affect the prosecutor's charging decision
15. (d) 600,000

Matching

1. F
2. G
3. A
4. E
5. D
6. H
7. C
8. B

CHAPTER TEN

PRETRIAL PROCEDURES

KEY TERMS AND CONCEPTS

Booking
Complaint
Indictment
Information
Arraignment
Nolo Contendere
Guity Plea
Not Guilty Plea
Plea-Bargaining
Bail
Bondsman
Eighth Amendment
Release on Recognizance
Manhattan Bail Project
Stack v. Boyle
Bail Reform Act
Pretrial Detention
Grand Jury
Presentment
True Bill
No Bill
Preliminary Hearing
Brady v. United States
Santobello v. New York
Bordenkircher v. Hayes
Pre-Pleading Investigation
Pretrial Settlement Conference
Pretrial Diversion
Continuance

FILL-IN REVIEW

1. When an individual is arrested on a misdemeanor charge, he or she is ordinarily ___________ from the police station to answer charges in ___________ at a subsequent date.

2. The accused who is arrested on a felony is usually ___________ by the police until ___________ at court.

3. An ____________ is a written accusation drawn up and submitted to the ____________ ____________ by the prosecutor charging an individual with a crime.

4. The ____________ is a charging document which does not use the grand jury to test its sufficiency, but rather uses a ____________ hearing, or a probable cause hearing.

5. ____________ represents money or some other security provided to the court in order to insure ____________ by the defendant in subsequent hearings.

6. The key issue in determining bail is founded on the ____________ that the defendant will appear at subsequent criminal proceedings.

7. The success of ROR programs resulted in further bail reforms culminating in the enactment of the federal ____________ ____________ Act of 1966.

8. The criminal defendant who is not eligible for ROR or bail is subject to ____________ detention.

9. The grand jury's functions are two-fold: ____________ and ____________.

10. If the grand jury fails to find probable cause, a ____________ bill is passed; conversely if probable cause exists, a ____________ bill is passed.

11. A grand jury is ordinarily comprised of ____________ to ____________ individuals, depending on the requirements of the jurisdiction.

12. A preliminary hearing is conducted before a ____________ and, unlike the grand jury hearing, the proceedings are ____________ to the public.

13. A unique aspect of the preliminary hearing is that the defendant has the alternative of ____________ the proceeding.

14. In most states, a guilty plea may be withdrawn and replaced with a ____________ ____________ plea at any point prior to ____________ if good cause is shown.

15. A plea of ____________, which is essentially a plea of guilty, may only be entered at the discretion of the ____________ and the prosecutor.

16. ______-______ represents a process whereby the defendant pleads guilty in exchange for a ____________ serious charge or for an agreement by the prosecutor to recommend a ____________ sentence.

17. The strength or weakness of the government's case is generally the major factor in the decision to ____________ or establish a ____________ agreement.

18. ____________ investigations are summaries of the case before a plea rather than after the plea is given to the court.

19. The pretrial ____________ conference is a method used to improve ____________ and fairness in plea-bargaining.

20. Without exception, diversion priority is given to ____________ offender ____________.

21. Diversion program involvement usually begins after arrest and ____________ of the individual, but before ____________.

SELF-TEST

True-False

1. Research in criminal justice indicates that virtually no relationship exists between release into the community and rates of failure to appear for trial.

2. An information is a charging document which makes use of the grand jury to test its sufficiency.

3. Bail may be denied at the indulgence of the court.

4. Many experts believe that money bail is an unsatisfactory pre-trial release procedure.

5. ROR allows for the release of a defendant without any requirements that he or she put up money bail.

6. Pre-trial custody accounts for more incarceration in the United States than does imprisonment after sentencing.

7. The grand jury usually meets at the request of the judge, moreover hearings are closed and secret.

8. The grand jury indicts almost all the cases presented to it.

9. An arraignment occurs subsequent to a grand jury or preliminary hearing.

10. Several constitutional rights are surrendered when an individual pleads guilty to a crime in court.

11. The highest probability of the acceptance of a plea bargain is where caseload pressures are greatest.

12. More than 40 percent of those held in local jails have been accused of crimes but have not been convicted.

13. For all practical purposes, plea-bargaining exists in all jurisdictions throughout the country.

14. A typical goal of a diversion program is to create effective resources where none exist.

15. Under the Bail Reform Act, assuring the appearance of defendants in court is the only legitimate concern of most release decisions.

Multiple Choice

1. When arrested on a felony charge, the accused is usually detained by the police until:
   a. arraignment
   b. pretrial hearings
   c. the accusatory pleading
   d. trial

2. The formal charging process for a felony may include:
   a. an indictment
   b. a complaint
   c. an information
   d. both a and c

3. The purpose of a ____________ is to require the prosecutor to present facts so that the judge can determine if the defendant should be held over for trial.
   a. preliminary hearing
   b. indictment
   c. plea bargaining
   d. none of the above

4. The right to pretrial freedom has been enunciated in the case of:
   a. _Brady v. United States_
   b. _Stack v. Boyle_
   c. _Bordenkircher v. Hayes_
   d. _Santobello v. New York_

5. With few exceptions, other than perhaps murder, all accused persons are entitled to bail that is not excessive, as stated in the ____________ Amendment.
   a. Fourth
   b. Fifth
   c. Sixth
   d. Eighth

6. The study of the Vera Institute's ROR program (the Manhattan Bail Project) revealed a default rate of less than:
   a. 1%
   b. 5%
   c. 10%
   d. 20%

7. When a grand jury fails to find probable cause, a __________ is passed.
   a. true bill
   b. presentment
   c. no contest
   d. no bill

8. A report from the grand jury containing information about its investigations and often a recommendation of indictment is known as:
   a. stare decisis
   b. nolo contendere
   c. presentment
   d. true bill

9. More than __________ of the defendants appearing before the court plead guilty prior to the trial stage.
   a. 90%
   b. 50%
   c. 75%
   d. 10%

10. When the defendant stands mute before the bench during an arraignment, a plea of __________ is entered.
   a. nolo contendere
   b. guilty
   c. not guilty
   d. guilty with an explanation

11. In which of the following court cases did the Supreme Court hold that the breaking of a plea bargain agreement, by the prosecutor, would result in reversal for the defendant:
   a. *Brady v. United States*
   b. *Santobello v. New York*
   c. *Betts v. New York*
   d. *Boykin v. Alabama*

12. It is basically the responsibility of the __________ to see that the accused understands the nature of the plea-bargaining process and the guilty plea.
   a. judge
   b. prosecutor
   c. defense attorney
   d. both a and c

13. In plea-bargaining, the defendant waives his right to a jury trial which is guaranteed by the __________ Amendment.
    a. Fourth
    b. Fifth
    c. Sixth
    d. Eighth

14. Candidates for diversion programs typically have had no more than __________ prior adult convictions.
    a. one
    b. two
    c. three
    d. five

15. In plea-bargaining, a defendant waives his privilege against self-incrimination which is guaranteed by the __________ Amendment.
    a. First
    b. Fourth
    c. Fifth
    d. Sixth

Matching

1. Indictment
2. Information
3. Bail
4. Arraignment
5. Plea-bargaining

A. Money or some other security provided to the court to insure the appearance of the defendant at every subsequent stage of the criminal justice process.

B. Process whereby the defendant pleads guilty in exchange for a lesser charge or for an agreement by the prosecutor to recommend a reduced sentence.

C. Charging document used in a preliminary hearing.

D. Court appearance at which the judge informs the defendant of the charges against him and appoints counsel if it has not yet been retained.

E. Written accusation drawn up and submitted to the grand jury by the prosecutor charging the person with a crime.

ESSAY QUESTIONS

1. What is the bail system and why is it considered to be unsatisfactory? Explain the recent and most major method of bail reform, describing who initiated it and why they did so.

2. What are the two main functions of the grand jury? What reports can be issued from each?

3. What are the legal consequences of a defendant's plea of guilty? What precautions must a judge take because of these?

4. Plea-bargaining is a widespread yet controversial aspect of the criminal justice system; what are the major advantages and disadvantages of this process?

5. Discuss the major advantages/disadvantages of the grand jury and preliminary hearing systems?

CHAPTER 10 ANSWER SECTION

FILL-IN REVIEW

1. released, court
2. detained, arraignment
3. indictment, grand jury
4. information, preliminary
5. Bail, appearance
6. probability
7. Bail Reform
8. pretrial
9. investigatory, accusatory
10. no, true
11. 16, 23
12. magistrate, open
13. waiving
14. not guilty, sentencing
15. nolo contendere, judge
16. Plea-bargaining, less, reduced
17. bargain, plea
18. Pre-pleading
19. settlement, visibility
20. first, misdemeanants
21. arraignment, trial

SELF-TEST

True-False

1. True
2. False
3. False
4. True
5. True
6. True
7. False
8. True
9. True
10. True
11. False
12. True
13. False
14. True
15. True

Multiple Choice

1. (a) arraignment
2. (d) both a and c
3. (a) preliminary hearing
4. (b) _Stack v. Boyle_
5. (d) Eighth
6. (a) 1%
7. (d) no bill
8. (c) presentment
9. (a) 90%
10. (c) not guilty
11. (b) _Santobello v. New York_
12. (d) defense attorney
13. (c) Sixth
14. (a) one
15. (c) Fifth

Matching

1. E
2. C
3. A
4. D
5. B

CHAPTER ELEVEN

THE COURTS

KEY TERMS AND CONCEPTS

Criminal Court
Defendants
Assembly-Line Justice
Courts of Limited Jurisdiction
Lower Courts
Courts of General Jurisdiction
Trial DeNovo
Appellate Courts
Court of Last Resort
State Supreme Court
U.S. District Courts
U.S. Circuit Courts
U.S. Supreme Court
Landmark Decision
Writ of Certiorari
Court Caseload
Judge
Charge the Jury
Jury Trial
Sentencing
Missouri Plan
Court Administration
Court Administrators
SEARCH
PROMIS

FILL-IN REVIEW

1. The court process is designed to provide an open and impartial forum for deciding the ___________ of a particular conflict between two or more parties.

2. Overloaded court dockets have given rise to charges of "assembly-line justice" in which a majority of defendants are induced to plead ___________, ___________ trials are rare, and the ___________ trial is a highly desired but unattainable concept.

3. Courts of ___________ jurisdiction handle the more serious ___________ cases while courts of ___________ jurisdiction handle ___________.

4. ___________ courts review the procedures of a case in order to determine whether an ___________ was made by judicial authorities.

5. The federal government has established a three-tier heirarchy of court jurisdiction, which in order of ascendancy consists of ___________ Courts, Courts of ___________, and the ___________ Court.

6. United States District Courts are the ___________ courts of the ___________ system.

7. The Federal Court of Appeals is also known as the ___________ court of appeals, of which there are ___________ in number.

8. The circuit court is empowered to review federal and state appellate court cases on ___________ and ___________ issues involving the rights guaranteed by the Constitution.

9. The U.S. Supreme Court is the nation's highest appellate body and the court of ___________ ___________ for all cases tried in the various federal and state courts.

10. The Supreme Court is composed of ___________ members appointed for life terms by the ___________ with approval of ___________.

11. When the U.S. Supreme Court decides to hear a case, it grants a writ of ___________.

12. A ___________ decision by the Supreme Court becomes a ___________ which must be honored by all lower courts.

13. The significant increase in both ___________ and ___________ litigation has forced state and local governments to allocate even greater ___________ to the courts.

14. A judge's sentencing discretion influences the ___________ and ___________ process.

15. A judicial selection method consisting of a three-part approach is known as the ___________ Plan.

16. While most states require that judges in appellate and general jurisdiction courts be ___________ and members in good standing of the state ___________, that is usually not the case for judges in the ___________ criminal courts.

17. The need for efficient management techniques in an ever-expanding criminal court system has led to the recognition of improved court ___________ as a possible device for relieving court ___________.

18. In larger court jurisdictions, the individuals in charge of court management are the court ___________.

19. In the past, LEAA has funded a fifty-state consortium for the purpose of establishing a standardized crime reporting system entitled ___________.

SELF-TEST

True-False

1. A majority of states use popular election as their method for judicial selection.

2. The jurisdiction of U.S. District Courts may overlap with that of state courts.

3. The federal Circuit Courts concentrate on constitutional issues rather than on the retrial cases.

4. Each individual state is allowed one U.S. District Court to handle the large amount of appeals.

5. Because of their overwhelming influence on the entire criminal justice system, all judges are required to have a college degree, though not necessarily a law degree.

6. Popular judicial elections can be conducted on a nonpartisan basis.

7. The Supreme Court may choose to hear only those cases that it deems important, appropriate, and worthy of its attention.

8. When the Supreme Court hands down a decision, its rule becomes a precedent which must be honored by all lower courts.

9. Appellate courts do not try cases.

10. Some states separate limited courts into those that handle criminal cases only and those that handle civil cases only.

11. The overwhelming majority of general jurisdiction courts hear only serious criminal matters.

12. Trial de novo means that on appeal an entirely new trial is granted.

13. Both criminal and civil litigation has significantly increased recently.

Multiple Choice

1. About ___________ of the courts of general jurisdiction also have the responsibility of reviewing cases on appeal from courts of limited jurisdiction.
   a. one-fourth
   b. one-half
   c. two-thirds
   d. three-fourths

2. Courts of limited jurisdiction include:
   a. probate courts
   b. juvenile courts
   c. family courts
   d. all of the above

3. Federal courts of appeals are sometimes referred to as:
   a. judicial courts
   b. district courts
   c. circuit courts
   d. none of the above

4. In which region of the country was the percentage increase in criminal cases the greatest?
   a. West
   b. Northeast
   c. South
   d. North central

5. Directly influenced by the judge's sentencing discretion are:
   a. the defense
   b. the police
   c. the prosecutor
   d. both b and c

6. Approximately ___________ of the states have established intermediate appellate courts to review decisions by trial courts and administrative agencies.
   a. one-third
   b. one-half
   c. two-thirds
   d. three-fourths

7. Courts of limited jurisdiction may also be known as:
   a. lower courts
   b. municipal courts
   c. traffic courts
   d. both a and b

8. A computer system is designed especially to help courts comply with the statutory time limits provision of the Speedy Trial Act of 1974 is:
   a. SEARCH
   b. PROMIS
   c. SPEEDY
   d. none of the above

9. Which of the following are <u>not</u> considered to be a part of the Missouri Plan to select judges:
   a. nonpartisan elections of incumbent judges
   b. judicial nominating commission
   c. elected offical appoints judges
   d. all of the above are included

10. Today there are approximately ____________ Federal District Courts.
   a. 50
   b. 75
   c. 95
   d. 120

11. At which state court level are the majority of serious criminal offenses tried:
   a. limited jurisdiction
   b. special jurisdiction
   c. general jurisdiction
   d. none of the above

12. The first state to implement most of the American Bar Association Standards by formal court rule was:
   a. Florida
   b. California
   c. North Dakota
   d. New York

13. There are ____________ federal appeals courts (circuit courts).
   a. 9
   b. 11
   c. 16
   d. 23

14. ____________ of all general jurisdiction courts hear serious felonies.
   a. 25%
   b. 50%
   c. 75%
   d. 95%

15. Which of the following courts is responsible for enforcing orders from federal administrative agencies:
   a. Federal Appeals Court
   b. Federal District Court
   c. U.S. Supreme Court
   d. court of claims

Matching

1.	SEARCH	A.	Statutory time limits
2.	De novo	B.	Trial courts
3.	Lower courts	C.	New trial
4.	Missouri Plan	D.	Assembly-line justice
5.	Courts of general jurisdiction	E.	Judicial selection
6.	PROMIS	F.	Serious criminal matters
7.	Court of last resort	G.	Appellate jurisdiction
8.	District Courts	H.	Standardized crime reporting

ESSAY QUESTIONS

1. What does the term "assembly-line justice" mean; what can be done about it?

2. Briefly describe what you consider to be the best method of judicial selection.

3. Discuss what is meant by a "landmark decision"; why are such decisions important?

4. Briefly describe the role of the court administrator and how technology can improve court management.

CHAPTER 11 ANSWER SECTION

FILL-IN REVIEW

1. justice
2. guilty, jury, speedy
3. general, felony, limited, misdemeanors
4. Appellate, error
5. District, Appeals, Supreme
6. trial, federal
7. circuit, eleven
8. substantive, procedural
9. last resort
10. nine, President, Congress
11. certiorari
12. landmark, precedent
13. criminal, civil, resources
14. arrest, charging
15. Missouri
16. attorneys, bar, lower
17. administration, congestion
18. administrators
19. SEARCH

SELF-TEST

True-False

1. True
2. True
3. True
4. False
5. False
6. True
7. True
8. True
9. True
10. True
11. False
12. True
13. True

Multiple Choice

1. (d) three-fourths
2. (d) all of the above
3. (c) circuit courts
4. (b) Northeast

5. (d) both b and c
6. (c) two-thirds
7. (d) both a and b
8. (b) PROMIS
9. (d) all of the above are included
10. (c) 95
11. (c) general jurisdiction
12. (a) Florida
13. (b) 11
14. (d) 95%
15. (a) Federal Appeals Court

Matching

1. H
2. C
3. D
4. E
5. F
6. A
7. G
8. B

CHAPTER TWELVE

THE CRIMINAL TRIAL

KEY TERMS AND CONCEPTS

Continuance
Sixth Amendment
Jury Trial
Duncan v. Louisiana
Baldwin v. New York
In re Oliver
Six-Person Jury
Apodica v. Oregon
Fourteenth Amendment
Powell v. Alabama
Gideon v. Wainwright
Argersinger v. Hamlin
Faretta v. California
Waiver
Klopfer v. North Carolina
Barker v. Wingo
Fixed Time Rule
Demand Waiver Rule
Speedy Trial Act
Adversary Proceeding
Venire
Voir Dire
Challenge of Cause
Peremptory Challenges
Direct Examination
Cross-Examination
Directed Verdict
Surrebuttal
Verdict
Hung Jury
Sentence
Douglass v. California
In Forma Pauperis
Proof Beyond a Reasonable Doubt
In re Winship

FILL-IN REVIEW

1. The adjudication state of the criminal justice process begins with a fact-finding hearing which seeks to determine the truth of the facts of a case before the court; this process is usually referred to as the ____________ ____________.

2. It appears that fewer than ____________ percent of all defendants ever reach the trial stage.

3. The defendant has the right to choose whether the trial will be before a ____________ or ____________.

4. Although the ____________ Amendment to the U.S. Constitution guarantees the defendant the right to a jury trial, the defendant can and often does ____________ this right.

5. In the case of Baldwin v. New York, the U.S. Supreme Court held that a defendant has a right to a ____________ trial when he faces a prison sentence of ____________ months or more.

6. One of the most important issues involving a jury trial has been the actual ____________ of the jury.

7. In the case of ____________, the U.S. Supreme Court held that a six person jury in a criminal trial did not deprive a defendant of his constitutional right to a jury trial.

8. In the Apodica v. Oregon case, the U.S. Supreme Court upheld an Oregon statute which required ____________ of ____________ jurors to convict the defendant.

9. In Gideon v. Wainwright, the U.S. Supreme Court stated that while the Sixth Amendment did not explicitly lay down a rule binding on the states, the ____________ to ____________ was so fundamental and ethical to a fair trial that is is made obligatory upon the states by the ____________ Amendment's due process clause.

10. The right to proceed ____________ ____________ is when the criminal defendant is guaranteed the right to be able to represent himself.

11. The time period measuring whether the defendant received a speedy trial attaches only after an ____________ or when ____________ charges are made.

12. The ____________ ____________ Act of 1974 guarantees the accused that the trial must be held within ____________ days after the arraignment.

13. ____________ are selected in both civil and criminal cases from tax assessments or voter registration lists in each court jurisdiction; this list is called a ____________ or jury array.

14. A ____________ ____________ proceeding involves the questioning of the jurors selected to determine their appropriateness to sit on the trial.

15. In addition to challenges for cause, both the prosecution and the defense are allowed ____________ ____________.

16. A ___________ verdict is a procedural device by means of which the ___________ attorney asks the judge to order the jury to return a verdict of not guilty.

17. In a criminal trial, the defendant is protected by the Fifth Amendment right to be free from ___________.

18. If a jury cannot reach a verdict, the trial may result in a ___________ ___________, and the prosecutor then has to bring the defendant to trial again if he desires a ___________.

19. The imposition of the criminal ___________ is normally the responsibility of the ___________ judge.

20. Proof beyond a ___________ ___________ is the standard required to convict a defendant charged with a crime at the adjuciatory stage of the criminal process.

SELF-TEST

True-False

1. According to Baldwin v. New York, a defendant has a constitutional right to a jury trial, even when the possible sentence is six months or less.

2. In most jurisdictions, there exists a direct criminal appeal to an appellate court as a matter of right.

3. In most states, imposition of the criminal sentence is normally the responsibility of the jury.

4. The continuance is a frequently-used disposition in which the court holds a case in abeyance without a finding of guilt in order to induce the accused to improve his behavior in the community.

5. Because only a small number of cases are actually tried by a jury, the trial process is no longer considered a central ingredient to the criminal justice system.

6. State courts must now provide counsel to indigent defendants for all criminal offenses whether or not there is a possibility of incarceration.

7. Today, most states and the federal government have statutes which fix the period of time in which an accused must be brought to trial.

8. The verdict by a jury in a criminal case must always be a unanimous one.

9. In Duncan v. Louisiana the U.S. Supreme Court held that the right to a trial by a jury was applicable to both the state and federal governemnts.

10. Peremptory challenges are not limited by law.

11. A directed verdict is a procedural device in which the prosecutor asks the judge to order the jury to return a verdict of guilty as charged.

12. Some jurisdictions have adopted the one-day one-trial jury system to increase the opportunity for a speedy trial.

13. In the case of _In re Winship_ held that both state and federal court systems were bound to grant public trials to criminal defendants.

14. The case of _Gideon v. Wainwright_ made it clear that a person charged with a felony in a state court had an absolute right to counsel.

Multiple Choice

1. No state provides for less than twelve jurors in:
   a. felony cases
   b. aggravated assaults
   c. rape cases
   d. capital cases

2. On appeal of which case did the U.S. Supreme Court hold that no person could be imprisoned for any offense unless he was offered representation at trial:
   a. _Argersinger v. Hamlin_
   b. _Gideon v. Wainwright_
   c. _Powell v. Alabama_
   d. _Betts v. Brady_

3. The ____________ Amendment guarantees that no state shall deprive a citizen of life, liberty or property without due process of law.
   a. Fourth
   b. Fifth
   c. Sixth
   d. Fourteenth

4. Less than ____________ of all criminal cases ever reach trial stage.
   a. 5%
   b. 15%
   c. 25%
   d. 50%

5. Under the Speedy Trial Act of 1974, from the point of arrest the accused must be brought to trial within ____________ days in the federal system.
   a. 30
   b. 60
   c. 100
   d. 150

6. What the witness say, heard, or touched himself is put forth as:
   a. evidence
   b. testimony
   c. examination
   d. opinion

7. Who generally enters a motion for a directed verdict:
   a. defense
   b. prosecution
   c. judge
   d. both b and c

8. The initial list from which jurors are selected is called a:
   a. voir dire
   b. venire
   c. pro se
   d. jury list

9. The right to be represented by counsel for defense is guaranteed by the ____________ Amendment.
   a. Fourth
   b. Fifth
   c. Sixth
   d. Fourteenth

10. A study conducted by the American Civil Liberties Union concluded that "misdemeanants represented by attorneys are ____________ times as likely to emerge from police court with all charges dismissed as are defendants without counsel".
   a. three
   b. five
   c. ten
   d. twenty

11. A defendant is protected from a second prosecution for the same offense (double jeopardy) by the ____________ Amendment.
   a. Fifth
   b. Sixth
   c. Eighth
   d. Fourteenth

12. Once the charge is given to the jury, they retire to deliberate upon a:
   a. sentence
   b. verdict
   c. conviction
   d. recommendation

13. Which of the following cases determined that the accused is entitled to a jury trial when the possible sentence is six months or longer:
    a. Duncan v. Louisiana
    b. Williams v. Florida
    c. Baldwin v. New York
    d. Gideon v. Wainwright

14. The Barker v. Wingo case is important because it rejects measuring a speedy trial by:
    a. fixed time period rule
    b. the demand for waiver rule
    c. the congested court rule
    d. both a and b

15. When the defendant is granted counsel at public expense because the court believes that he or she has meritorious appeal, this is known as:
    a. in loco parentis
    b. pro se
    c. voir dire
    d. in forma pauperis

16. In a criminal trial when the judge instructs the jury as the principles of law, this is known as:
    a. charge
    b. directs
    c. surrebuttal
    d. hung jury

Matching

1.	Faretta v. California	A.	Right to a speedy trial.
2.	In re Oliver	B.	Right to self-representation.
3.	In re Winship	C.	Right to a public trial.
4.	Douglas v. California	D.	Right to counsel at trial.
5.	Gideon v. Wainwright	E.	Right to a jury trial.
6.	Klopfer v. North Carolina	F.	Right to counsel on a direct first appeal.
7.	Duncan v. Louisiana		
		G.	Proof beyond a reasonable doubt.

ESSAY QUESTIONS

1. Discuss the significance of the following U.S. Supreme Court cases: Powell v. Alabama, Gideon v. Wainwright, and Argersinger v. Hamlin.

2. What are the four primary purposes of the right to a speedy trial? What factors must be considered in determining whether or not this right has been violated?

3. Explain the difference between challenges for cause and peremptory challenges in the jury selection process.

4. In your opinion, what is the importance of the reasonable doubt standard for establishing guilt?

5. Outline the major stages in a criminal trial. Explain why you would rather have a court or jury trial.

CHAPTER 12 ANSWER SECTION

FILL-IN REVIEW

1. criminal trial
2. 5
3. judge, jury
4. Sixth, waive
5. jury, six
6. size
7. <u>Williams</u> <u>v.</u> <u>Florida</u>
8. 10, 12
9. right, counsel, Fourteenth
10. pro se
11. arrest, formal
12. Speedy Trial, 60
13. Jurors, venire
14. voir dire
15. peremptory challenges
16. directed, defense
17. self-incrimination
18. hung jury, conviction
19. sentence, trial
20. reasonable doubt

SELF-TEST

True-False

1. False
2. True
3. False
4. True
5. False
6. False
7. True
8. False
9. True
10. False
11. False
12. True
13. False
14. True

Multiple Choice

1. (d) capital cases
2. (a) Argersinger v. Hamlin
3. (d) Fourteenth
4. (a) 5%
5. (c) 100
6. (b) testimony
7. (a) defense
8. (b) venire
9. (c) Sixth
10. (b) five
11. (a) Fifth
12. (b) verdict
13. (c) Baldwin v. New York
14. (d) both a and b
15. (d) in forma pauperis
16. (a) charge

Matching

1. B
2. C
3. G
4. F
5. D
6. A
7. E

CHAPTER THIRTEEN

SENTENCING

KEY TERMS AND CONCEPTS

Retaliation
Lex Talionis
Punishment
Retribution
Rehabilitation
Deterrence
Fine
Tate v. Short
Probation
Habitual Offender Statutes
Sexual Psychopath Statutes
Incarceration
Determinacy
Capital Punishment
Furman v. Georgia
Gregg v. Georgia
Cruel and Unusual Punishment
Eighth Amendment
Indeterminate Sentence
Model Sentencing Act
Model Penal Code
Indefinite Sentence
Determinate Sentence
Fixed Term
Definite Sentence
Flat-time
Mandatory Sentences
Presumptive Sentencing
Good-time
Pre-Sentence Report
Sentencing Counsils
Appellate Review
Retributive Model
Just Deserts

FILL-IN REVIEW

1. In the early stages of Western society, the primary purpose for punishing an individual for wrongdoing was __________ rather than __________ of further criminal behavior.

2. The basis for retaliation was the well-known principle of "___________ ___________".

3. ___________ reflects the belief that the punishment of a guilty offender will serve as an example to others.

4. The four different kinds of sentences or dispositions which the court may impose upon the offender after conviction are a ___________, ___________ sentence, ___________, or ___________.

5. Beginning in the middle of the twentieth century and continuing up through the present, many people feel that ___________ should be the primary purpose of the criminal ___________.

6. The U.S. Supreme Court in Tate v. Short recognized that imprisoning a person unable to pay a ___________ discriminates against the ___________.

7. The most common sentence in the American judicial system is ___________, where the ___________ is permitted to live in the community subject to compliance with legally imposed conditions.

8. The ___________ imposed are a critical factor in probation.

9. The sentence of ___________ is imposed when the general public must be protected from further ___________ activity by the defendant.

10. In the 1980's there seems to be a more conservative, "get tough" approach to ___________, and particularly ___________.

11. In 1972 the U.S. Supreme Court in Furman v. Georgia decided that the discretionary imposition of the death penalty was ___________ and ___________ punishment under the ___________ and ___________ Amendments of the Constitution.

12. In 1976, the Supreme Court ruled in Gregg v. Georgia that the statute which held that the finding by a jury of at least one "___________ ___________" out of ten is required in pronouncing the death penalty in murder cases.

13. As a result of the Furman decision, there has been an ___________ in the number of persons sentenced to death each year.

14. When a convicted offender is to be sentenced to prison, the ___________ of a jurisdiction provide the possible ___________ that may be imposed by the court.

15. The indeterminate sentence describes a situation where there is a ___________ sentence but either no term or a different ___________ term that the prisoner must complete before becoming eligible to leave the institution.

16. The determinate/definite sentence originally was developed to impose ___________ sentences equally on all those convicted of a similar ___________.

17. The reasons that "there is no such thing as a determinate or definite sentence in this country" is due to the fact that all states have some ___________ programs which ___________ the portion of time served by the defendant.

18. Sentencing ___________ are meetings of judges who sit regularly in a particular court to discuss the appropriate disposition of defendants who are awaiting ___________.

19. One of the major concerns resulting from extreme judicial ___________ is the degree to which ___________ exists in the sentencing process.

20. ___________ sentencing generally limits the judge's discretionary power to impose any disposition but that which is authorized by the ___________.

21. ___________ sentencing would allow the legislature to set a minimum and maximum term for a particular crime, with the judge setting a ___________ or ___________ sentence within this range.

22. ___________ ___________ credits are provided to inmates in most states and the federal system by legislation; their development was based on the idea that a system of ___________, rather than punishment, would be more effective in controlling inmate's behavior.

23. The "___________ ___________" concept rejects the idea of individualized sentences based on the particular offender and adopts the position that sentences should be imposed with regard to the ___________ of the offense.

SELF-TEST

True-False

1. Some states exclude offenders convicted of certain offenses from being placed on probation.

2. The most common sentence given to convicted offenders is incarceration.

3. Today, there is no such thing as an actual determinate or definite sentence in America.

4. A fine generally may not be combined with other sentencing alternatives.

5. The Model Penal Code recommends providing a separate sentencing approach for dangerous offenders.

6. Mandatory sentencing generally does not limit the judge's discretionary power to impose any disposition but that authorized by the legislature.

7. Probation is a sentence in itself.

8. Studies on the impact of capital punishment on the murder rate indicated that it has a significant effect as a deterrent measure.

9. The length of time served by an inmate is controlled by the correctional agency in indeterminate sentences.

10. In most jurisdictions, the good time allowance covers the entire period of incarceration.

11. Most states have a true indeterminate criminal sentence.

12. Presumptive sentencing allows the legislature to set a fixed or determinate sentence for a particular crime.

13. Today there seems to be a conservative, "get tough" approach to sentencing, particularly incarceration.

Multiple Choice

1. In early colonial times, the primary purpose for imposing punishment on the convicted was:
   a. rehabilitation
   b. retribution
   c. reintegration
   d. restriction

2. One of the major concerns resulting from extreme judicial discretion is the degree to which ___________ exists in the sentencing process.
   a. distress
   b. duress
   c. disparity
   d. difficulty

3. A meeting of judges to discuss special problems related to sentencing is known as a:
   a. sentencing council
   b. sentencing institute
   c. appellate review of sentences
   d. both b and c

4. The case of ___________ recognized that imprisoning a person unable to pay a fine discriminates against the poor.
   a. *Jurek v. Texas*
   b. *Tate v. Short*
   c. *Roberts v. Roberts*
   d. *Lockett v. Ohio*

5. Which of the following terms attempts to eliminate sentencing disparity:
   a. determinate sentence
   b. just deserts
   c. retributive justice model
   d. all of the above

6. Indeterminate sentences are the heart of what model of corrections:
   a. treatment
   b. punishment
   c. retribution
   d. reintegration

7. The American Law Institute's Model Penal Code reduces all crimes to ____________ grades of felony and ____________ grades of misdemeanor.
   a. 5, 4
   b. 3, 3
   c. 3, 2
   d. 2, 4

8. Even today, no more than ____________ of the states review the merits of a sentence upon appeal.
   a. one-fourth
   b. one-third
   c. one-half
   d. two-thirds

9. The predominant form of sentence used in the criminal process is the:
   a. indeterminate sentence
   b. determinate sentence
   c. mandatory sentence
   d. both b and c

10. The U.S. Supreme Court decided that discretionary imposition of the death penalty was cruel and unusual in:
   a. *Gregg v. Georgia*
   b. *Jurek v. Texas*
   c. *McGinnis v. Royster*
   d. *Furman v. Georgia*

11. Which of the following cases determined that a convicted offender can be sentenced to death when one or more "aggravating circumstances" were involved:
   a. *Furman v. Georgia*
   b. *Gregg v. Georgia*
   c. *Roberts v. Louisiana*
   d. *Proffitt v. Florida*

12. The current sentencing reform suggestions seem to emphasize __________ sentences.
    a. increasing
    b. decreasing
    c. standardizing
    d. both b and c

13. Under indeterminate sentencing, the actual length of time served by the inmate is controlled by the:
    a. judge
    b. correction agency
    c. legislature
    d. both a and b

14. Presumptive sentencing attempts to:
    a. limit judicial discretion
    b. reduce sentencing disparity
    c. impose a sentence which must be served
    d. all of the above

Matching

1.	Rehabilitation	A.	Lex talionis
2.	Determinate sentence	B.	Treatment
3.	Retaliation	C.	Fear of punishment
4.	Recidivist	D.	Habitual offender
5.	Deterrence	E.	Fixed time
6.	Reduced sentence	F.	Good time

ESSAY QUESTIONS

1. Briefly explain the four major types of sentencing. Which is the most common? What basic criteria do most judges examine in determining the type and length of a sentence?

2. What are the major arguments regarding our approach to the "dangerous offender"? What tends to happen to the not-so-dangerous offender? What characteristics of our laws allow these things to happen?

3. What was the significance of the Supreme Court decision concerning capital punishment in 1972? In 1976? What is your opinion of capital punishment and why?

4. Discuss the basic pros and cons of mandatory sentences.

5. Explain a major difficulty concerning sentencing councils.

CHAPTER 13 ANSWER SECTION

FILL-IN REVIEW

1. retaliation, prevention
2. lex talionis
3. Deterrence
4. fine, suspended, probation, incarceration
5. rehabilitation, sentence
6. fine, poor
7. probation, offender
8. conditions
9. incarceration, criminal
10. sentencing, incarceration
11. cruel, unusual, Eighth, Fourteenth
12. aggravating circumstance
13. increase
14. statutes, penalties
15. maximum, minimum
16. specific, offense
17. parole, shorten
18. counsils, sentencing
19. discretion, disparity
20. Mandatory, legislature
21. Presumptive, fixed, determinate
22. Good time, rewards
23. "just deserts", seriousness

SELF-TEST

True-False

1. True
2. False
3. True
4. False
5. True
6. False
7. True
8. False
9. True
10. False
11. False
12. False
13. True

Multiple Choice

1. (b) retribution
2. (c) disparity
3. (b) sentencing institute
4. (b) Tate v. Short
5. (d) all of the above
6. (a) treatment
7. (c) 3, 2
8. (c) one-half
9. (a) indeterminate sentence
10. (d) Furman v. Georgia
11. (b) Gregg v. Georgia
12. (d) both b and c
13. (b) correction agency
14. (d) all of the above

Matching

1. B
2. E
3. A
4. D
5. C
6. F

CHAPTER FOURTEEN

PROBATION

KEY TERMS AND CONCEPTS

Probation
Judicial Reprieve
Recognizance
Sureties
John Augustus
Federal Criminal Code
Federal Probation Statute
Shock Probation
Split Sentences
Model Penal Code
Restitution
Standard Rules
Chief Probation Officer
Probation Officers
Intake
Diagnosis
Rule Enforcer
Social Worker
Civil Servant
Traditionalist
Team Player
Pre-Sentence Investigations
Pre-Trial Programs
Volunteers
Intensive Supervision
Probation Subsidy
Probation Revocation
<u>Gagnon</u> <u>v.</u> <u>Scarpelli</u>

FILL-IN REVIEW

1. Probation is the practice of maintaining ____________ criminal offenders in the ____________ under supervision of ____________ authority.

2. ____________ were people who made themselves responsible for the behavior of the offender after they were ____________.

3. ____________ ____________ of Boston is usually credited with organizing the modern probation concept.

4. The term of a probationary sentence may extend to the limit of the ___________ prison term, or the court may set a time limit that reflects the ___________ period.

5. The combining of probation with jail sentences is known as ___________ ___________ or ___________ ___________.

6. The extensive use of probation is probably a reflection of its low ___________ and its importance to the efficient ___________ of the justice system.

7. Many states have attempted to control judicial ___________ by creating ___________ for granting probation.

8. A probation sentence is usually viewed as an act of ___________ on the part of the court, and is reflective of the ___________ aspects of the criminal justice system.

9. A presiding judge may not impose capricious or cruel conditions, such as requiring an offender to make ___________ out of ___________ to the seriousness of his or her criminal act.

10. In addition to ___________ rules, judges may legally impose restrictions on a probationer tailored to fit his or her individual needs and to protect ___________ from additional harm.

11. ___________ is a process by which probation officers ___________ cases that have been summoned to the court for initial appearances.

12. ___________ is the analysis of the probationer's personality and the subsequent development of a personality ___________ that may be helpful in treating the offender.

13. The treatment function is a product of both the ___________ and ___________ aspect of probation.

14. The ___________ ___________ style of probation is primarily concerned with maintaining the best interests of the community; the opposite style is that of ___________ ___________, whole total concern is with the client.

15. The ___________ ___________ style differs from the other probation styles in its efforts to heed the skills and personal characteristics of the offender in formulating the treatment plan.

16. ______-______ ___________ are reports used by the court in making decisions whether to grant probation, incarcerate, or use other forms of treatment.

17. It is generally believed that the two most important factors influencing the probation officer's investigation report are the nature of the current ___________ and the offender's criminal ___________.

18. The ___________ concept requires defendants to either pay back the victims of crime or serve the community for their ___________ acts.

19. Today, it has become common practice for probation departments to employ ___________ and ___________ in what might be considered regular hire positions.

20. Probation ___________ involves the grant of state financial aid to local probation departments so that they can institute special services for offenders who would otherwise be sent to ___________.

21. The Gagnon v. Scarpelli case held that both probationers and parolees have a constitutionally limited right to ___________ in ___________ proceedings.

SELF-TEST

True-False

1. Most evidence suggests that shock probation tends to be more effective than regular probation.

2. The original enthusiasm for the concept of restitution has been dampened by concern that it has not lived up to its promise as an alternative to incarceration.

3. The right to counsel in revocation proceedings differs for probationers and parolees.

4. Intake is most common in the juvenile justice process, but may also be employed in adult felony cases.

5. An offender's probation cannot be revoked unless he commits another crime.

6. In some states, jail terms can actually be a condition of probation.

7. As it is practiced today, probationary rules may actually impede the probationer's achieving the goals of treatment.

8. The problems associated with the Social Work style involve the quality of the relationship to the client.

9. In dealing with clients, the Civil Servant style of probation places a maximum amount of attention on rules, therapy, etc.

10. Restitution programs normally require offenders to pay back victims of crime (or serve the community) as a condition of probation.

11. The philosophy of probation is that the average offender is not actually a dangerous criminal or menance to society.

12. National evaluations of volunteer programs indicate that they are about as successful as traditional approaches.

13. The rate of probation usage is generally stable from state to state.

Multiple Choice

1. The analysis of the probationer's personality and the subsequent development of a personality profile which may be helpful in treating the offender is known as:
   a. diversion
   b. determination
   c. diagnosis
   d. discretion

2. The probation officer whose style is that of Social Worker has as his or her main concern the:
   a. society
   b. rules
   c. position
   d. client

3. Probation along with a monetary fine is often imposed for:
   a. juveniles
   b. first offenders
   c. while-collar crimes
   d. misdemeanors

4. A process by which probation officers interview cases which have been summoned to the court for an initial appearance is known as:
   a. diagnosis
   b. intake
   c. investigation
   d. diversion

5. In practice, ___________ states today provide counsel to indigent defendants at probation revocation hearings.
   a. very few
   b. 25%
   c. 50%
   d. almost all

6. The typical ___________ program requires probationers to meet with their supervisors almost daily.
   a. intensive supervision
   b. probation subsidy
   c. split sentence
   d. both a and b

7. The ___________ type of probation officer regards probation as a "privilege, not a right".
   a. Rule Enforcer
   b. Traditionalist
   c. Team Player
   d. Civil Servant

8. The originator of the modern concept of probation was:
   a. David Rothman
   b. O.W. Wilson
   c. John Augustus
   d. none of the above

9. The practice of ___________ enabled convicted offenders to remain free if they agreed to enter into a debt obligation with the state.
   a. probation
   b. recognizance
   c. judicial reprieve
   d. sureties

10. There are approximately ___________ adult probation agencies in the United States.
   a. 500
   b. 1,000
   c. 2,000
   d. 5,000

11. During the course of a probationary term, a violation of the rules of probation or the commission of a new crime can cause probation to be:
   a. renewed
   b. revoked
   c. reorganized
   d. recalled

12. Which of the following cases held that both probationers and parolees have a constitutionally limited right to counsel:
   a. *Morrissey v. Brewer*
   b. *United States v. Reed*
   c. *Mempa v. Rhay*
   d. *Gagnon v. Scarpelli*

13. The probation style in which the officer "plays it by ear" is known as:
   a. Traditionalist
   b. Civil Servant
   c. Team Player
   d. Social Worker

14. The Federal Criminal Code recommends that probation for felons last ___________ years.
    a. three
    b. five
    c. seven
    d. three to seven

15. It has been estimated that the probation department's recommendation on sentencing is followed in about ___________ of the cases.
    a. 25%
    b. 50%
    c. 75%
    d. 95%

Matching

1. Restitution
2. Intake
3. Diagnosis
4. Rule Enforcer
5. Civil Servant
6. Traditionalist
7. Social Worker

A. Payback victims or serve the community.

B. Probation style where self-interest is the primary concern.

C. Interview of cases which have been summoned to the court for initial appearance.

D. Probation style where officer is experience oriented.

E. An analysis of the probationer's personality.

F. Probation style primarily concerned with maintaining the best interests of the community.

G. Probation style where primary concern is with the client.

ESSAY QUESTIONS

1. Why do many experts disapprove of combining probation with jail sentences and why do so courts allow it anyway?

2. Discuss the major duties of a probation officer; should these be expanded or narrowed?

3. Discuss the major reasons why a court may decide not to grant probation.

4. Discuss the procedural safeguards for probation revocation; from what cases were these safeguards denied?

5. Give several reasons why restitution should or should not be required of criminal offenders.

CHAPTER 14 ANSWER SECTION

FILL-IN REVIEW

1. convicted, community, court
2. Sureties, released
3. John Augustus
4. suspended, sentencing
5. shock probation, split sentences
6. cost, operation
7. discretion, guidelines
8. clemency, rehabilitative
9. restitution, proportion
10. standard, society
11. Intake, interview
12. Diagnosis, profile
13. investigative, diagnostic
14. Rule Enforcer, Social Worker
15. Team Player
16. Pre-sentence investigations
17. offense, history
18. restitution, criminal
19. paraprofessionals, volunteers
20. subsidy, prison
21. counsel, revocation

SELF-TEST

True-False

1. False
2. True
3. False
4. False
5. False
6. True
7. True
8. True
9. False
10. True
11. True
12. True
13. False

Multiple Choice

1. (c) diagnosis
2. (d) client
3. (c) white-collar crimes
4. (b) intake
5. (d) almost all
6. (a) intensive supervision
7. (a) Rule Enforcer
8. (c) John Augustus
9. (b) recognizance
10. (c) 2,000
11. (b) revoked
12. (d) Gagnon v. Scarpelli
13. (a) Traditionalist
14. (b) five
15. (d) 95%

Matching

1. A
2. C
3. E
4. F
5. B
6. D
7. G

CHAPTER FIFTEEN

AN OVERVIEW OF CORRECTIONAL HISTORY AND INSTITUTIONS

KEY TERMS AND CONCEPTS

Corrections
Jails
Prisons
Incapacitation
Wergild
Capital Punishment
Corporal Punishment
Poor Laws
William Penn
Society for Alleviating the Miseries of Public Prisons
Walnut Street Jail
Auburn System
Pennsylvania System
Contract System
Convict-Lease System
State Account System
Mutual Welfare League
County Jail
Custodial Convenience
Maximum Security
Medium Security
Mimimum Security
Community Corrections
Halfway House

FILL-IN REVIEW

1. The term corrections refers to the entire range of ___________ and/or ___________ options available to the offender.

2. Prisons are more suited to control, ___________, and ___________ than to rehabilitation and treatment.

3. A popular notion is that prisons are places of ___________ in which offenders who harmed innocent people are kept apart from society.

4. During the middle ages the Roman custom of settling disputes by fine, known as ____________, was adopted as a means of resolving interpersonal conflicts.

5. ____________ ____________ developed in the early seventeenth century required that the poor, vagrants, and vagabonds be put to work in public or private enterprise.

6. The U.S. correctional system had its origin in Pennsylvania under the leadership of ____________ ____________.

7. In the Walnut Street Jail most prisoners were placed in ____________ cells, where they remained in ____________ and solitude and did not have the right to work.

8. The philosophy of the ____________ system was crime prevention through fear of ____________ and silent confinement.

9. In 1818, the state of ____________ took the radical step of establishing a prison that placed each inmate in a ____________ cell and did not provide them with any ____________ to do.

10. During the civil war era, prison ____________ developed and became the main theme around which institutions were ____________.

11. The greatest significance of Z.R. Brockway's contributions was the injection of a degree of ____________ into the industrial prisons of that day.

12. As the mid-1980's approach, the nation's correctional policy seems to be to keep ____________ offenders out of the system and to incarcerate dangerous offenders for ____________ periods of time.

13. Jails have two major purposes: the ____________ of accused offenders prior to trial, and reform and correction of offenders convicted of ____________.

14. Because jails are almost always administered on a ____________ level, there has been neither significant regulation of services nor development of a unified national policy to meet adequate jail ____________.

15. Jails are usually administered under the concept of "____________ ____________" which involves giving inmates minimum ____________ of treatment and benefits while controlling the cost of jail operations.

16. The Commission on ____________ for ____________ is attempting to improve jail conditions by setting up standards on health care and treatment.

17. Prisons are generally organized or classified on three levels--____________, ____________, or ____________--and each has its own distinctive characteristics.

18. The byword of the ___________ security prison is security.

19. A major concern of criminal justice policy makers has been the rapid ___________ in the nation's prison ___________.

20. A facility that maintains an offender just prior to release is known as a ___________ ___________; it attempts to bridge the gap between ___________ living and the ___________.

SELF-TEST

True-False

1. Community treatment in corrections has come into prominence in the last 15 years.

2. America's inmate population has been on the increase since the early 1970's.

3. In the Auburn System, the key to prison discipline was punishment.

4. Evaluation of specific halfway house programs has indicated strong support for this type of treatment.

5. The incapacitation or "just deserts" approach to penal philosophy has become virtually obsolete in American courts and correctional systems.

6. Medium security prisons, like maximum security prisons, are surrounded by walls.

7. Minorities account for a disproportionate percentage of the daily jail population.

8. It is estimated that recidivism rates may actually exceed 80 percent.

9. The Walnut Street Jail instituted the congregate system, where most prisoners ate and worked in groups.

10. Jails sometimes serve as institutions of reform and correction for offenders convicted of felonies.

11. The average stay in jail is brief.

12. Minimum security prisons operate without armed guards or walls.

13. The Pennsylvania system placed each inmate in a single cell and provided them with work to do.

Multiple Choice

1. Jails are usually administered under the concept of:
   a. custodial convenience
   b. correctional service
   c. preventive detention
   d. security maintenance

2. When officials sold the labor of inmates to private business, this was known as a:
   a. state account system
   b. convict-lease system
   c. contract system
   d. none of the above

3. Which of the following modern trends is <u>not</u> applicable to today's correctional system:
   a. violence within the system
   b. control and punishment emphasis
   c. litigation by inmates seeking greater rights
   d. all of the above are applicable

4. According to recent statistics, approximately ____________ percent of inmates in the nation's jails are unconvicted:
   a. 10%
   b. 25%
   c. 50%
   d. 60%

5. The philosophy of crime prevention in the Auburn System was:
   a. fear of punishment
   b. silence/isolation
   c. physical torture
   d. both a and b

6. Typically, jails are under the jurisdiction of ____________ government.
   a. city
   b. county
   c. state
   d. federal

7. There are approximately ____________ jails in the United States.
   a. 1,000
   b. 2,500
   c. 3,500
   d. over 5,000

8. A 1978 jail census found that about ___________ percent of jails had no rehabilitation personnel on their staffs:
   a. 25%
   b. 50%
   c. 75%
   d. 90%

9. Which of the following conditions helps explain the significant rise in prison population:
   a. increased birth rate
   b. state lawmakers increasing penalties
   c. high unemployment rate
   d. both b and c

10. In today's larger prisons, most are similar to the:
    a. Auburn System
    b. Eastern System
    c. Walnut System
    d. Pennsylvania System

11. In 1787, the "Philadelphia Society for Alleviating the Miseries of Public Prisons" was formed by the:
    a. Mormons
    b. Quakers
    c. Mennonites
    d. Moonies

12. Perhaps the most common occupants of minimum security prisons are:
    a. misdemeanants
    b. white-collar criminals
    c. bank robbers
    d. auto thieves

13. The underlying motive(s) of banishment in historical Europe was:
    a. punishment
    b. economic
    c. rehabilitation
    d. both a and b

14. If the current incarceration rate continues to increase, the correctional population may reach ___________ by 1985:
    a. 150,000
    b. 250,000
    c. 500,000
    d. over one million

Matching

1.	Halfway House	A.	Z.R. Brockway
2.	Prison	B.	Congregate System
3.	Walnut Street Jail	C.	Single Cell Habitation
4.	Auburn Prison	D.	Community Correction
5.	Pennsylvania System	E.	Quakers
6.	Elmira Prison	F.	Incapacitation
7.	Punishment Reform	G.	Solitary Cells

ESSAY QUESTIONS

1. Describe the Auburn System; what characteristics of this system remain in our prisons today?

2. Explain the philosophy of "custodial convenience".

3. What is the difference between maximum, medium, and minimum security prisons?

4. What is your opinion of community corrections; should they be used more to reduce overcrowding in prisons?

5. If you were a county sheriff, what steps would you take to improve the operation and maintenance of your jail facility?

CHAPTER 15 ANSWER SECTION

FILL-IN REVIEW

1. treatment, punishment
2. punishment, security
3. incapacitation
4. wergild
5. Poor Laws
6. William Penn
7. solitary, isolation
8. Auburn, punishment
9. Pennsylvania, single, work
10. industry, organized
11. humanitarianism
12. nonthreatening, long
13. detention, misdemeanors
14. county, conditions
15. custodial convenience, standards
16. Accreditation, Corrections
17. maximum, medium, minimum
18. maximum
19. increase, population
20. halfway house, institutional, community

SELF-TEST

True-False

1. True
2. False
3. False
4. False
5. False
6. True
7. True
8. True
9. False
10. False
11. True
12. True
13. False

Multiple Choice

1. (a) custodial convenience
2. (c) contract system
3. (d) all of the above are applicable
4. (d) 60%
5. (d) both a and b
6. (b) county
7. (c) 3,500
8. (c) 75%
9. (d) both b and c
10. (a) Auburn System
11. (b) Quakers
12. (b) white-collar criminals
13. (d) both a and b
14. (c) 500,000

Matching

1. D
2. F
3. G
4. B
5. C
6. A
7. E

CHAPTER SIXTEEN

INSTITUTIONAL LIFE

KEY TERMS AND CONCEPTS

Prison Overcrowding
Total Institutions
Hustling
Niche
Inmate Subculture
Social Code
Argot
Prisonization
"Right Guy"
"Square Johns"
"Con Politicians"
"Outlaws"
Importation Model
Thief Subculture
Convict Subculture
Less Eligibility
Counseling
Vocational Training
Educational Training
Work Release
Conjugal Visits
Coed Prisons
Prison Industries
Make-Believe Family
Self-Governance

FILL-IN REVIEW

1. There are approximately ___________ prison facilities in the United States.

2. Prison "___________" is a form of black market involving the sale of illegal commodities.

3. An inmate's ___________ is a kind of insulation from the pains of imprisonment.

4. The ___________ and final phase of the prison cycle begins when the sentence nears its end and a ___________ date is in sight.

5. Passed on from one generation of inmates to another, the inmate ___________ ___________ represents the values of interpersonal relations within the prison.

6. Prisoners have a unique language or ___________ which they use.

7. An inmates assimilation into the existing prison culture is know as the ___________ process.

8. The term for an inmate who conforms to the rules of the inmate culture is the "___________ ___________".

9. The ___________ model suggests that the inmate ___________ is actually imported from the outside world.

10. Irwin and Cressey found that the inmate world was divided into three groups, each corresponding to a role in the outside world: the ___________ subculture, the ___________ subculture, and the ___________ culture.

11. The philosophy of ___________ ___________ has been interpreted to mean that prisoners should always be treated less well than the most underprivileged _____-_____ citizen.

12. A beneficial feature of ___________ counseling is the use of ___________ treatment personnel as group leaders.

13. In addition to individual analysis and group processes, inmate rehabilitation may also be pursued through ___________ or ___________ training.

14. _____-_____ programs allow deserving inmates to leave the institution and hold regular jobs in the ___________.

15. ___________ services help inmates create job plans essential to receiving parole and to be successfully reintegrated into the community.

16. During ___________ visits prisoners are able to have completely ___________ meetings with wives and family on a regular basis.

17. Most prominent among traditional prison ___________ are those designed to help maintain and run the ___________ and provide services for other public or state facilities.

18. The majority of ___________ institutions are ___________, similar to college dormitories and other group homes in the community.

19. A form of adaptation to prison used by women is the ___________ ___________ family, containing masculine and feminine figures acting as fathers and mothers.

20. Prison ___________ and ___________ are everpresent features of institutional life.

21. A recent trend in prisons which may be associated with violence is the ___________ caused by rapid increases in the prison ___________.

SELF-TEST

True-False

1. The prison cycle contains four major phases.

2. Many heterosexual men will turn to homosexual relationships when faced with long sentences in prison.

3. Surveys have indicated that not one state has avoided crowding inmates in less than adequate space.

4. One of the problems associated with conjugal visition is that appropriate facilities are almost universally lacking.

5. Scientific evaluation of work release programs indicates that they tend to be effective in reducing recidivism rates.

6. Today, almost every state has at least one institution with a work-release program.

7. Fortresslike prisons holding more than 1,000 inmates are still predominate in the U.S.

8. It is quite likely that there is a correlation between prison overcrowding and violence.

9. Opposition from organized labor ended the profitability of commercial prison industries.

10. The characteristics of prison inmates are fairly typical of the general U.S. population.

11. Conjugal visitation is more frequently used in Latin America and Europe than in the U.S.

12. A common practice among female inmates is "carving".

13. States that administer coed programs generally do not view them as being successful.

Multiple Choice

1. Inmates who conform to the rules of the inmate culture are identified by which of the following roles:
   a. "conformers"
   b. "right guys"
   c. "square Johns"
   d. both a and b

2. Violation of prison rules may result in disciplinary action against the inmate, which may have an effect on:
   a. good time
   b. transfer
   c. privileges
   d. all of the above

3. Females constitute about ___________ percent of the total prison population:
   a. 4%
   b. 10%
   c. 15%
   d. 20%

4. Most prison experts agree that a minimum of ___________ square feet is needed for each prison inmate.
   a. 30
   b. 50
   c. 60
   d. 90

5. Irwin and Cressey found that the ___________ subculture always try to "do their own time":
   a. convict
   b. thief
   c. conventional
   d. none of the above

6. The inmate ___________ represents the values of interpersonal relations within the prison:
   a. subculture
   b. argot
   c. social code
   d. prisonization

7. The ___________ phase of the prison cycle is a low energy period when the inmate becomes a fixture within the institutional community.
   a. first
   b. second
   c. third
   d. fourth

8. There are approximately ___________ prison facilities in the U.S.
   a. 250
   b. 570
   c. 680
   d. 870

9. Which of the following characteristics is not typical of the prison inmate:
   a. middle-aged
   b. undereducated
   c. recidivist
   d. minority

10. Most of the existing research on inmate culture ignores the issue of:
   a. class
   b. race
   c. age
   d. education

11. A survey of the nation's prison systems indicate that ___________ percent of the inmates had no income during the 12 months prior to their arrest.
   a. 5
   b. 10
   c. 15
   d. 20

12. A recent survey of women's prisons indicated that:
   a. vocational programs were oriented toward traditional "female roles"
   b. most had basic educational programs
   c. most had advanced educational programs
   d. all of the above

13. Prison violence is primarily thought to occur because:
   a. inhuman conditions convert men to violence
   b. inmates are often violence-prone individuals
   c. prison mismanagement leads to such behavior
   d. all of the above

14. While black citizens make up about 12 percent of the population, they account for ___________ percent of those in prison.
   a. 25
   b. 37
   c. 48
   d. none of the above

Matching

1.	Hustle	A.	Violence
2.	Argot	B.	Self-mutilation
3.	Prisonization	C.	Unwritten guidelines
4.	Work-release	D.	Furlough
5.	Carving	E.	Hidden economy
6.	Overcrowding	F.	Inmate assimilation
7.	Social code	G.	Inmate language

ESSAY QUESTIONS

1. Briefly describe the three cycles of attitude and behavior change through which an inmate passes.

2. What is the philosophy of "less eligibility"? Should this philosophy be followed?

3. Give several reasons why prison industries should or should not be given high priority.

4. Discuss several explanations regarding the causes of prison violence. What, if anything, can be done to alleviate such violence?

CHAPTER 16 ANSWER SECTION

FILL-IN REVIEW

1. 568
2. hustling
3. niche
4. third, release
5. social code
6. argot
7. prisonization
8. right guy
9. importation, subculture
10. thief, convict, conventional
11. less eligibility, law-abiding
12. group, nonprofessional
13. vocational, educational
14. Work-release, community
15. Employment
16. conjugal, private
17. industries, institution
18. women's, nonsecure
19. make believe
20. violence, brutality
21. overcrowding, population

SELF-TEST

True-False

1. False
2. True
3. True
4. True
5. False
6. True
7. True
8. True
9. True
10. False
11. True
12. True
13. False

Multiple Choice

1. (b) "right guys"
2. (c) all of the above
3. (a) 4%
4. (c) 60
5. (b) thief
6. (c) social code
7. (b) second
8. (b) 570
9. (a) middle-aged
10. (b) race
11. (d) 20
12. (d) all of the above
13. (d) all of the above
14. (c) 48

Matching

1. E
2. G
3. F
4. D
5. B
6. A
7. C

CHAPTER SEVENTEEN

PAROLE

KEY TERMS AND CONCEPTS

Parole
Parole Board
Parole Rules
Parolee
Parole Officers
Technical Parole Violation
Transportation
Property in Service
Indentured Servant
Alexander Maconochie
Sir Walter Crofton
Guardians
Parole Grant Hearing
Presumptive Parole Date
Greenholtz v. Inmates of Nebraska Penal and Correctional Complex
Connecticut Board of Pardons v. Dumschat
Parole Prediction
Salient Factor Score Index
Parole Supervision Styles
Technical Violator
Shock Parole
Parole Revocation
Morrissey v. Brewer
Post-Release Aftercare

FILL-IN REVIEW

1. Parole is the planned community ___________ and supervision of incarcerated offenders prior to the actual expiration of their ___________ sentences.

2. The decision to parole is determined by ___________ requirement, usually involving completion of a ___________ sentence; the granting of parole is usually made by a parole ___________.

3. If a ___________ violates the rules, he or she can be returned to the institution to serve the remainder of the sentence; this is known as a ___________ parole violation.

4. The parole process contains elements of two conflicting orientations; these are ___________ and ___________.

5. In 1717 the British Parliament passed legislation creating the concept of ___________, where control of prisoners was transferred to a contractor until the expiration of their sentences.

6. Alexander ___________ instituted reforms such as classification and rehabilitation programs, which became models for the ___________ of convicted offenders.

7. In the United States, the concept of releasing inmates into the community before expiration of their sentence can be traced to the first "___________ ___________" developed in ___________ ___________ in 1917.

8. The first "real" parole program was initiated around 1822 by volunteers from the ___________ society for Alleviating the Miseries of ___________ ___________.

9. Two factors influence the parole rate: prison ___________ and length of the ___________ term.

10. The actual parole decision is made at a parole ___________ ___________.

11. A new approach to selecting inmates for parole is the concept of the ___________ parole ___________; the offender is notified of the date within ___________ days of the start of his or her prison term.

12. In <u>Greenholtz</u>, the U.S. Supreme Court held that parole was a ___________ and not a ___________, and that inmates are not entitled to receive a full compliment of ___________ ___________ rights.

13. Of primary concern to the parole board when considering parole is whether the inmate can make an adequate ___________ to the community and refrain from further ___________ activity.

14. The ___________ ___________ score is used as a predictive aid composed of seven elements that are used to estimate the probability of an inmate returning to crime if released.

15. Parole ___________ may curtail or prohibit certain types of ___________ while encouraging or demanding others.

16. Parole ___________ often begins in the institution when institutionally based agents help the inmate create his parole ___________.

17. The ___________ parole officer is the guardian of middle-class community morality.

18. NCCD researchers have found that offenders who had committed the most ___________ offenses were most likely to be ___________ on parole.

19. Immediate short-term incarceration for parole violators to impress them with the seriousness of a violation is called ___________ ___________.

20. The parole ___________ process is almost always started by the parole ___________ who believes that the parolee has violated a parole condition, or when the parolee has been charged with a new ___________.

21. The Morrissey v. Brewer case held that the ___________ Amendment requirement of ___________ ___________ of law actually applied to the parole ___________ process.

22. Proponents of presumptive or _____-_____ sentencing have called for abolition of parole, they believe inmates should be sentenced to a ___________ number of years.

23. A number of states that adopted presumptive sentencing models retain parole as a form of _____-_____ ___________.

SELF TEST

True-False

1. In the late nineteenth century in the United States, "rehabilitated" offenders were released early under the supervision of paid citizens known as guardians.

2. Research appears to be mixed regarding the effectiveness of parole as a rehabilitation tool.

3. In some states, officers have combined caseloads of probation and parole clients.

4. The Protective Agent utilizes direct assistance, lecturing, praise, and blame in supervising a parolee.

5. The adequancy of a parole plan is an important element in the board's decision to grant community release.

6. Representation by an attorney is a parolee's right at a revocation hearing.

7. The parole officer may have to play a much greater role in directing and supervising the lives of his clients than is required of the probation officer.

8. Prediction tables make use of information on past parole cases to predict the probable success of current ones.

9. In the early 1700's in Britain, transportation became the most common sentence for murderers.

10. Parole is the planned community release and supervision of offenders before any of their prison sentence has been served.

11. The salient factor score index is currently used in all federal parole decision making.

12. Proponents of flat-time sentencing support the abolition of parole.

13. Recent national studies have indicated that adult parole is more effective than had been expected.

14. There is a standard national policy to guide the way inmates are informed of a parole board's decisions.

Multiple Choice

1. The only state to completely abolish all forms of parole is:
   a. Maine
   b. Colorado
   c. Arizona
   d. California

2. Shock parole involves immediate ___________ incarcerations for violators to impress them with the seriousness of the violation.
   a. intermediate-term
   b. medium-term
   c. short-term
   d. long-term

3. Regarding parole revocation, a parolee has a right to:
   a. advance written notice of charges
   b. call witnesses on his or her behalf
   c. a hearing before a neutral hearing board
   d. all of the above

4. Which of the following cases was concerned with inmate rights at parole hearings:
   a. *Morrissey v. Brewer*
   b. *Greenholtz v. Inmates of the Nebraska Penal and Corrections Complex*
   c. *Munks v. New Jersey Board of Parole*
   d. both a and b

5. Which of the following elements determines eligibility for parole:
   a. minimum sentence served
   b. accumulated good time
   c. policy of the parole board
   d. both a and c

6. It is estimated nationally that approximately __________ of all inmates are eventually granted parole.
   a. 30%
   b. 50%
   c. 70%
   d. 80%

7. The style of parole supervision where the officer shifts back and forth in taking sides with the offender and the community is the __________.
   a. Punitive Officer
   b. Protective Officer
   c. Welfare Worker
   d. Political Opportunist

8. The parole revocation process is almost always initiated by:
   a. the police
   b. the parole officer
   c. the parole board
   d. the parold agent

9. Parole board members in the majority of jurisdictions are appointed by:
   a. civil service lists
   b. the president's commission
   c. the governor
   d. the prison warden

10. Which supervision style is most likely to coerce the offender into conformity:
   a. Punitive Officer
   b. Protective Agent
   c. Welfare Worker
   d. Political Opportunist

11. According to the National Council on Crime and Delinquency, which offender group has the most successful parole outcome:
   a. forcible rape
   b. motor vehicle thefts
   c. manslaughter
   d. homicide

12. The most well known parole prediction device is the:
   a. recidivism rate
   b. base expectancy score index
   c. salient factor score index
   d. parole plan

13. Almost __________ of the parole boards require no particular qualifications for members.
   a. one-fourth
   b. one-third
   c. one-half
   d. three-fourths

Matching

1.	Client oriented	A.	Parole hearing rights
2.	Sir Walter Crofton	B.	Parole prediction
3.	_Greenholtz v. Inmates of Nebraska_	C.	Parole eligibility procedure
4.	_Morrissey v. Brewer_	D.	Punitive officer
5.	Salient factor score	E.	Due process in parole revocation
6.	Presumptive Parole Date	F.	Welfare worker
7.	Offender Conformity	G.	Private volunteers
8.	Alexander Maconochie	H.	Classification Programs

ESSAY QUESTIONS

1. What are the primary functions of a parole board?
2. What qualifications would be important for members of a parole board in your opinion?
3. What are the primary considerations taken into account by a parole board in determining release?
4. Do you think that parole boards should have greater or less discretion? Explain.
5. Discuss the significance of the _Morrissey v. Brewer_ case.

CHAPTER 17 ANSWER SECTION

FILL-IN REVIEW

1. release, prison
2. statutory, minimum, board
3. parolee, technical
4. treatment, enforcement
5. property in service
6. Maconochie, treatment
7. good-time laws, New York
8. Philadelphia, Public Prisons
9. population, supervisory
10. grant hearing
11. presumptive, date, 120
12. privilege, right, due process
13. adjustment, criminal
14. salient factor
15. rules, behavior
16. supervision, plan
17. Punitive
18. serious, successful
19. shock parole
20. revocation, officer, crime
21. Fourteenth, due process, revocation
22. flat-time, fixed
23. post-release, aftercare

SELF TEST

True-False

1. False
2. True
3. True
4. True
5. True
6. True
7. True
8. True
9. False
10. False
11. True
12. True
13. True
14. False

Multiple Choice

1. (a) Maine
2. (c) short-term
3. (d) all of the above
4. (b) <u>Greenholtz v. Inmates of the Nebraska Penal and Corrections Complex</u>
5. (d) both a and c
6. (c) 70%
7. (b) Protective Officer
8. (b) the parole officer
9. (c) the governor
10. (a) Punitive Officer
11. (d) homicide
12. (c) salient factor score index
13. (c) one-half

Matching

1. F
2. G
3. A
4. E
5. B
6. C
7. D
8. H

CHAPTER EIGHTEEN

PRISONERS' RIGHTS

KEY TERMS AND CONCEPTS

Hands-Off Doctrine
Federal Civil Rights Act
Cooper v. Pate
Ex parte Hull
Jailhouse Lawyer
Rose v. Lundy
Smith v. Wade
Substantive Rights
Procunier v. Martinez
Black Muslum
Class Actions
Exceptional Circumstances Doctrine
Newman V. Alabama
Estelle v. Gamble
Double-Bunking
Holt v. Sarver
Bell v. Wolfish
Rhodes v. Chapman
Procedural Rights
Wolff v. McDonnell
Inmate Grievance Committee
Jones v. North Carolina Prisoners Labor Union
Inmate Union
Attainder
Civil Rights
"Civil Death"

FILL-IN REVIEW

1. Prior to 1960, it was accepted that on conviction an individual forfeited all ___________ that were not expressly granted by statutory ___________ or correctional ___________.

2. The ____-______ doctrine is a policy whereby states and federal courts were reluctant to intervene in the operations of prisons.

3. Today, the ___________ ___________ ___________ Act serves as the fundamental basis on which courts have cautiously opened their doors to prisoner rights cases.

4. In the 1964 case of Cooper v. Pate the U.S. Supreme Court ruled that inmates who were being denied the right to practice their ___________ were entitled to legal redress under 42 U.S.C. ___________.

5. The 1941 Supreme Court case of Ex parte ___________ declared that access to the courts for an inmate was a basic constitutional right.

6. An inmate who offers skilled legal advice to another inmate is known as a ___________ ___________.

7. The expansion of prisoners' access to the courts has been limited by recent actions of the conservative ___________ court.

8. The term ___________ rights may be defined as privileges given to an individual through a statuatory or ___________ law.

9. In the ___________ case, prison officials were substantially restricted in their ___________ of prisoners' mail due to the decision of the Supreme Court.

10. ___________ freedom was the first area in which the courts lifted the hands-off doctrine; this action can be attributed to the ___________ ___________ movement in prisons.

11. Prior to the 1970's, the courts maintained their distance in medical rights cases through the creation of the ___________ ___________ doctrine.

12. In the Newman case, the entire ___________ prison system's ___________ facilities were declared inadequate.

13. In recent years, state and federal courts have placed strict limits on ___________ methods that may be considered ___________.

14. In the 1981 case of Rhodes v. Chapman the U.S. Supreme Court refused to ban the practice of _____-_____.

15. When inmates break prison rules, they are subject to ___________ measures within the institution.

16. In the ___________ case, the Supreme Court established precisely the constitutional safeguards required in prisons at a disciplinary proceeding.

17. In many prisons, ___________ ___________ committees have been set up to review accusations against guards, other inmates, and general prison living conditions.

18. Under the common law of ___________, convicted felons forfeited their land and possessions and their ___________ ___________.

19. Courts have considered individual requests by convicted felons to have their ___________ restored on a ___________ basis.

20. When "___________ ___________" statutes have been challenged, state and federal courts have ruled they are denial of due process and equal protection rights.

SELF TEST

True-False

1. A trend toward limiting the rights of prisoners has been established by the current U.S. Supreme Court.

2. The device most widely used to bring prisoners' complaints before state and federal courts was the Federal Civil Liabilities Act.

3. Cruel and unusual punishment has never been specifically defined by the U.S. Supreme Court.

4. In most states today, the restriction on voting rights of convicted offenders have been eliminated.

5. Inmates have a right to legal assistance of a jail house lawyer when filing civil rights actions against prison officials.

6. Courts have ruled that solitary confinement and corporal punishment are cruel and unusual.

7. The issue of prisoner's rights is not a new concept in the study of criminal justice.

8. Although Ex parte Hull granted inmates access to the courts, this right proved to be more theoretical than practical.

9. An inmate may hold any belief he wants, but may be denied some specific religious practices.

10. The procedural rights granted inmates have varied from case to case and jurisdiction to jurisdiction.

11. Since the 1970's, the courts have maintained their distance in medical rights cases through the exceptional circumstances doctrine.

12. It is widely believed that inmate grievance procedures can help to control violence.

13. While Smith v. Lundy is based on procedural technicalities, it should serve to slow down the number of prisoner's cases brought before the federal courts.

Multiple Choice

1. Which of the following cases dealt with mail censorship of inmates:
   a. Sostre v. McGinnis
   b. Wolff v. McDonnel
   c. Procunier v. Martinez
   d. Sostre v. Rockefeller

2. In what area did the courts first lift the hands-off doctrine:
   a. freedom of press
   b. freedom of religion
   c. freedom to medical treatment
   d. freedom from cruel and unusual punishment

3. For what right did the courts use the "exceptional circumstances" doctrine in order to maintain their distance:
   a. freedom of press
   b. freedom from cruel and unusual punishment
   c. right to medical treatment
   d. freedom of religion

4. What is the basis for prisoner right cases in the courts:
   a. Federal Civil Rights Act
   b. procedural rights
   c. Eighth Amendment
   d. hands-off doctrine

5. The concept of cruel and unusual punishment is founded in the ____________ Amendment.
   a. First
   b. Fifth
   c. Eighth
   d. Fourteenth

6. Under the hands-off doctrine, unless the circumstances of a case clearly indicated a serious breach of ____________ rights, the courts would avoid dealing with correctional administrative matters.
   a. First Amendment
   b. Fifth Amendment
   c. Eighth Amendment
   d. Fourteenth Amendment

7. Which of the following cases applied procedural safeguards to prison discipline:
   a. Sostre v. Rockefeller
   b. Procunier v. Martinez
   c. Bell v. Wolfish
   d. Wolff v. McDonnel

8. The Supreme Court has ruled that "failure or refusal to provide medical care, or treatment so cursory as to amount to no treatment at all," may in the case of serious medical problems violate the ___________ Amendment.
   a. First
   b. Fifth
   c. Eighth
   d. Fourteenth

9. Freedom of expression is a right granted to individuals through the ___________ Amendment of the Constitution.
   a. First
   b. Fifth
   c. Eighth
   d. Fourteenth

10. When the hands-off doctrine was finally lifted, this action could be attributed to the growing influence of the ___________ in the prisons.
   a. Quakers
   b. Adventist supporters
   c. Black Muslims
   d. Eastern Hindus

11. In most jurisdictions, a criminal record disqualifies an individual from:
   a. marrying
   b. becoming divorced
   c. adopting children
   d. burial

12. At what state prison did the court find the overall prison conditions so deplorable that they were constitutionally unacceptable?
   a. Nebraska
   b. Alabama
   c. Mississippi
   d. Arkansas

13. Although ___________ applied to the narrow issue of religious freedom, it opened the door to providing other rights for inmates:
   a. *Johnson v. Avery*
   b. *Cooper v. Pate*
   c. *Haines v. Kerner*
   d. *Rose v. Lundy*

Matching

1.	Hands-off doctrine	A.	Loss of civil rights
2.	*Bell v. Wolfish*	B.	Individual privileges granted by law
3.	*Newman v. Alabama*	C.	Opened door to providing rights for inmates
4.	Exceptional Circumstances Doctrine	D.	Prison conditions constitutionally unacceptable
5.	*Holt v. Sarver*	E.	Government restrictions can be used for legitimate purpose
6.	Substantive rights	F.	Reluctance of courts to intervene in prison matters
7.	Civil death	G.	Total disregard of human dignity
8.	*Cooper v. Pate*	H.	Medical facilities declared inadequate

ESSAY QUESTIONS

1. According to the National Advisory Commission, what were the three basic justifications for the courts' neglect of prison conditions? How have they changed since the 1960's?

2. Briefly discuss each of the four issues concerning substantive rights of prisoners; what Amendments guarantee these rights?

3. What constitutes cruel and unusual punishment? Explain what types of prison issues have typically been concerned with this question.

4. Discuss the significance and ramifications of the *Cooper v. Pate* and *Rhodes v. Chapman* cases.

5. List and explain five rights which are now or were once lost to the convicted offender; should such rights be restored upon completion of a sentence?

CHAPTER 18 ANSWER SECTION

FILL-IN REVIEW

1. rights, law, policy
2. hands-off
3. Federal Civil Rights
4. religion, 1983
5. Hull
6. jailhouse lawyer
7. Burger
8. substantive, constitutional
9. Procunier, censorship
10. Religious, Black Muslum
11. exceptional circumstances
12. Alabama, medical
13. disciplinary, inhumane
14. double-bunking
15. disciplinary
16. Wolff
17. inmate grievance
18. attainder, civil rights
19. rights, case-by-case
20. civil death

SELF TEST

True-False

1. True
2. False
3. True
4. True
5. True
6. False
7. False
8. True
9. True
10. True
11. False
12. True
13. False

Multiple Choice

1. (c) <u>Procunier v. Martinez</u>
2. (b) freedom of religion
3. (c) right to medical treatment
4. (a) Federal Civil Rights Act
5. (c) Eighth
6. (c) Eighth
7. (d) <u>Wolff v. McDonnel</u>
8. (d) Fourteenth
9. (a) First
10. (c) Black Muslums
11. (c) adopting children
12. (d) Arkansas
13. (b) <u>Cooper v. Pate</u>

Matching

1. F
2. E
3. H
4. G
5. D
6. B
7. A
8. C

CHAPTER NINETEEN

JUVENILE JUSTICE

KEY TERMS AND CONCEPTS

Parens Patriae
Poor Laws
Apprenticeship
Chancery Court
Childsavers
Illinois Juvenile Court Act
Delinquent Children
Status Offenders
PINS
CHINS
In re Gault
Fare v. Michael C.
California v. Prysock
Intake
Detention
Diversion
Waiver
Kent v. United States
Breed v. Jones
In re Winship
"Preponderance of the Evidence"
McKeiver v. Pennsylvania
Disposition
Post-disposition
Inmates v. Affleck
Morales v. Turman
Nelson v. Heyne

FILL-IN REVIEW

1. The philosophy of ___________ ___________ refers to the state acting in the interest of the child on behalf of the parent.

2. Since the mid-1960's, both the Warren and the Burger courts have taken a ___________ ___________ approach to juvenile law.

3. ___________ Laws allowed for the appointment of overseers to bind out destitute or neglected children as ___________.

4. One of the most concrete examples of institutional care for juveniles in early America was the ____________ of ____________.

5. The first comprehensive juvenile court was developed in ____________ in 1899.

6. Until 1967, judgments about children's actions and consideration for their ____________ ____________ were secondary.

7. Today's juvenile court system embodies both ____________ and ____________ orientations.

8. Juvenile court ____________ is established by state statute and is based on several factors, the first of which is ____________.

9. Having once obtained jurisdiction of a child, the court ordinarily retains it until the child reaches a specified age, usually the age of ____________.

10. The ____________ decision gave juveniles similar procedural safeguards as adults at trial proceedings, including the right to ____________, the right to confront ____________, and the privilege against _____-_____, and has indirectly influenced and reinforced juvenile *Miranda* rights.

11. In the *Fare* decision, the U.S. Supreme Court found that considering the "____________ of the ____________" the police had made a reasonable attempt to inform the suspect of his rights.

12. The ____________ stage represents an opportunity to place a child in ____________ programs both within the court and in the community.

13. After a juvenile is taken into custody, a decision is usually made whether to release the child to the parent or guardian or ____________ the child in a shelter pending ____________.

14. A federally sponsored study found that children confined in adult institutions were ____________ times as likely to commit ____________ as those placed in detention centers exclusively for juveniles.

15. ____________ refers to the process of screening out children from the juvenile court without judicial determination.

16. Today most jurisdictions provide by statute for ____________, or transfer, of juvenile offenders to the ____________ courts.

17. The U.S. Supreme Court in ____________ held that the waiver proceeding was a critically important stage in the juvenile process and that juveniles must be afforded ____________ requirements of due process of law at such proceedings.

18. There has been a trend toward giving __________ jurisdiction for __________ juvenile crimes to the adult courts and then allowing __________ the power to waive deserving cases back to the juvenile authorities.

19. In the landmark case of __________, the U.S. Supreme Court ruled that the concept of fundamental __________ be made applicable to juvenile delinquency proceedings.

20. In the __________ case, the U.S. Supreme Court held that the standard in a criminal prosecution of "__________ beyond a __________ __________" is also required in the adjudication of a delinquency petition.

21. Most formal dispositions used in the juvenile court include __________ and __________.

22. Standards for the juvenile justice system set forth by the American Bar Association suggest to a shift in juvenile court philosophy, from traditional __________ to the concept of "__________ __________".

23. The __________ case is significant because it was the first federal court of appeals decision to affirm a constitutional right to __________.

SELF TEST

True-False

1. The philosophy of the juvenile court is still based on the idea of *parens patriae*.

2. By 1925 most states had developed juvenile courts.

3. Status offenders are youths who engage in acts that are considered in violation of the penal code.

4. The practice of detaining juveniles in adult jails still continues today.

5. Approximately one-half of the states have passed laws that give adult courts original jurisdiction for many offenses committed by juveniles.

6. Delinquents and status offenders are frequently held in joint custody.

7. The term "intake" refers to the informal processing of cases by the juvenile court.

8. The right to receive *Miranda* warnings is applicable to juveniles as well as to adults.

9. Nominal sanctions deal primarily with such regulations as probation, restitution and counseling programs.

10. Unlike the adult where the sole criteria for pretrial release is availability for trial, the juvenile may be detained for other reasons, including his own protection.

11. Juvenile courts deal only with conduct of delinquent behavior.

12. Juveniles do not have due process rights in probation or parole revocation proceedings.

13. Plea bargaining is a fairly common practice in the juvenile justice system.

14. Most states have specific statutory provisions distinguishing the arrest process for children from that of adults.

Multiple Choice

1. The intake process serves which of the following functions:
   a. screens out cases not within the court's jurisdiction
   b. obtains assistance from the community
   c. reduces court demands
   d. all of the above

2. Court-based diversion programs have been used extensively for children who are:
   a. status offenders
   b. minor first offenders
   c. major first offenders
   d. both a and b

3. Which of the following cases instilled in juvenile proceedings the development of due process standards at the pretrial, trial and post-trial stages:
   a. Kent v. United States
   b. In re Gault
   c. In re Winship
   d. Morales v. Turman

4. Trends in juvenile sentencing include all but which of the following:
   a. removal of status offenders from juvenile system
   b. "just deserts" philosophy
   c. dispositions based on indeterminate sentencing
   d. passage of more harsh laws.

5. During the 1960's, the one exception in rights given to juveniles was:
   a. right to counsel
   b. right to jury trial
   c. right to cross-examine witnesses
   d. right to protection against double jeopardy

6. Which of the following cases held that trial by jury in juvenile court's adjudicative stage is not a constitutional requirement:
   a. _Kent v. United States_
   b. _In re Winship_
   c. _In re Gault_
   d. _McKeiver v. Pennsylvania_

7. What disposition is most commonly used in juvenile court:
   a. dismissal
   b. probation
   c. suspended judgment
   d. diversion

8. What of the following case(s) held that institutionalized juveniles have a statutory right to treatment:
   a. _Inmates v. Affleck_
   b. _Nelson v. Heyne_
   c. _Morales v. Turman_
   d. all of the above

9. At what stage in juvenile court proceedings must a writ of habeas corpus be filed:
   a. trial
   b. adjudication
   c. disposition
   c. post-disposition

10. The majority of the courts hold that a juvenile does _not_ have the right to:
    a. due process
    b. bail
    c. counsel
    d. ability to confront witnesses

11. When a juvenile is transferred to criminal court, it is called:
    a. waiver
    b. diversion
    c. disposition
    d. parens patriae

12. Which of the following cases dealt with the waiver process for juveniles:
    a. _People v. Overton_
    b. _Kent v. United States_
    c. _In re Winship_
    d. none of the above

13. The first separate juvenile court system was established in:
    a. New York
    b. California
    c. Illinois
    d. Massachusetts

14. Which of the following states opened the first institution for the reform of juveniles:
    a. New York
    b. Massachusetts
    c. Illinois
    d. California

15. Less than ___________ percent of all juveniles who are arrested and brought to court actually proceed to trial.
    a. 25
    b. 50
    c. 60
    d. 75

16. A federally sponsored study found that children confined in adult institutions were ___________ times as likely to commit suicide as those placed in detention centers exclusively for juveniles.
    a. two
    b. five
    c. eight
    d. twenty

Matching

1.	Parens patriae	A.	Right to treatment
2.	Waiver	B.	State acting in the interest of the child in parent's behalf.
3.	Status offender	C.	Commit an act in violation of the penal code.
4.	Delinquent children	D.	Incorrigible children.
5.	_In re Winship_	E.	Transfer from juvenile court to adult court.
6.	_In re Gault_	F.	Fundamental fairness.
7.	_Inmates v. Affleck_	G.	Beyond a reasonable doubt.

ESSAY QUESTIONS

1. Discuss the nature and significance of "status" offenses.

2. What three factors establish court jurisdiction over a juvenile?

3. What is waiver of jurisdiction? Under what conditions should juveniles be processed in adult courts?

4. Discuss the significance of the *In re Gault* case.

5. Describe the various dispositional alternatives available to the juvenile court and the recent trends in juvenile sentencing.

CHAPTER 19 ANSWER SECTION

FILL-IN REVIEW

1. parens patriae
2. due process
3. Poor, servants
4. House, Refuge
5. Illinois
6. constitutional rights
7. rehabilitative, legalistic
8. jurisdiction, age
9. majority
10. *Gault*, counsel, witnesses, self-incrimination
11. totality, circumstances
12. intake, informal
13. detain, trial
14. eight, suicide
15. Diversion
16. waiver, criminal
17. *Kent*, minimum
18. original, serious, judges
19. *In re Gault*, fairness
20. *Winship*, proof, reasonable, doubt
21. probation, commitment
22. rehabilitation, "just deserts"
23. *Nelson*, treatment

SELF TEST

True-False

1. False
2. True
3. False
4. True
5. True
6. True
7. False
8. True
9. False
10. True
11. False
12. True
13. False
14. False

Multiple Choice

1. (d) all of the above
2. (d) both a and b
3. (b) *In re Gault*
4. (c) dispositions based on indeterminate sentencing
5. (b) right to jury trial
6. (d) *McKeiver v. Pennsylvania*
7. (b) probation
8. (d) all of the above
9. (d) post-disposition
10. (b) bail
11. (a) waiver
12. (b) *Kent v. United States*
13. (c) Illinois
14. (b) Massachusetts
15. (b) 50
16. (c) eight

Matching

1. B
2. E
3. D
4. C
5. G
6. F
7. A

†